T0250442

TEAM PLANNING
FOR PROJECT
MANAGERS AND
BUSINESS ANALYSTS

ESI International Project Management Series

Series Editor
J. LeRoy Ward, Executive Vice President
ESI International, Arlington, Virginia

Team Planning for Project Managers and Business Analysts
Gail Levitt • 978-1-4398-5543-0

Practical Project Management for Building and Construction
Hans Ottosson • 978-1-4398-9655-6

Project Management Concepts, Methods, and Techniques
Claude H. Maley • 978-1-4665-0288-8

PgMP® Exam: Practice Test and Study Guide, Third Edition
Ginger Levin, and J. LeRoy Ward
978-1-4665-1362-4

Program Management Complexity: A Competency Model
Ginger Levin, and J. LeRoy Ward
978-1-4398-5111-1

Project Management for Healthcare
David Shirley • 978-1-4398-1953-1

Managing Web Projects
Edward B. Farkas • 978-1-4398-0495-7

Project Management Recipes for Success
Guy L. De Furia • 978-1-4200-7824-4

A Standard for Enterprise Project Management
Michael S. Zambruski • 978-1-4200-7245-7

Determining Project Requirements
Hans Jonasson • 978-1-4200-4502-4

The Complete Project Management Office Handbook, Second Edition
Gerard M. Hill • 978-1-4200-4680-9

Other ESI International Titles Available
from Auerbach Publications, Taylor & Francis Group

PMP® Challenge! Fourth Edition
J. LeRoy Ward and Ginger Levin • 978-1-8903-6740-4

PMP® Exam: Practice Test and Study Guide, Seventh Edition
J. LeRoy Ward • 978-1-8903-6741-1

The Project Management Drill Book: A Self-Study Guide
Carl L. Pritchard • ISBN: 978-1-8903-6734-3

Project Management Terms: A Working Glossary, Second Edition
J. LeRoy Ward • ISBN: 978-1-8903-6725-1

TEAM PLANNING FOR PROJECT MANAGERS AND BUSINESS ANALYSTS

Gail Levitt

CRC Press is an imprint of the
Taylor & Francis Group, an **informa** business
AN AUERBACH BOOK

PMBOK® Guide, PMI®, Project Management Institute®, and PMP® are registered trademarks of the Project Management Institute.

CRC Press
Taylor & Francis Group
6000 Broken Sound Parkway NW, Suite 300
Boca Raton, FL 33487-2742

© 2013 by Taylor & Francis Group, LLC
CRC Press is an imprint of Taylor & Francis Group, an Informa business

No claim to original U.S. Government works

International Standard Book Number: 978-1-4398-5543-0 (Hardback)

Visit the Taylor & Francis Web site at
http://www.taylorandfrancis.com

and the CRC Press Web site at
http://www.crcpress.com

Dedication

It takes great imagination for project professionals to develop teams to reach their true potential. The practical constraints of deadlines, budget, and scope can easily demand their full attention to focus on project deliverables in the present and rob them of important time needed to plan for the team's future. Even so, there are individuals with the vision and the drive to succeed as team developers. I know them as the bright lights of the 20,400 project managers and business analysts I have instructed, coached, and mentored since 1995. These are the individuals who stood out to me in the crowd as determined to develop their teams systematically to function more productively in their organizations. Whether or not they had formal authority over the teams they wanted to develop, these individuals shared two important characteristics: understanding the importance of creating, implementing, and communicating a team development plan while also lacking the knowledge and resources to develop their teams efficiently and effectively.

This book is dedicated to these project professionals; they already have the imagination and just need the tools, tips, and templates to achieve their visions. I would like to acknowledge the following people who inspired me at every step in the book writing process:

George Geniev, visionary thinker
Marilyn Levitt, role model
Karen Morris, team mediator
Rod Landgraff, strategic mentor
Phyllis Harber-Murphy, editor and administrator extraordinaire

Contents

Foreword

Through team work, ordinary people can produce extraordinary results. They can lift things that come into their hands a little higher; a little further on toward the heights of excellence.

—**Henry Ford**

Today, most businesses face the challenges of tough global competition, economic uncertainties, and limited access to personnel with the appropriate mix of skills, experiences, and cultural diversity to complete projects successfully. Their survival and growth in this competitive marketplace will depend on how effectively they manage their people, not just individually, but in teams—the backbone of project management. It is well recognized that teamwork leads to higher performance, especially when projects require agility, multidisciplinary skills, and appropriate judgments to operate within time and budget constraints. The effective management of these human resources is vital for creating high-performance teams.

A high-performance team is an energetic group of people committed to achieving a common vision and clear objectives, interdependent on one another, working well together, sharing responsibilities, and producing high-quality results. The success of projects, and hence the entire organization, depends upon the quality of the team's work. It is important to combine the appropriate level of resources with sufficient management support to do team planning because, as the saying goes, "if you fail to plan, you plan to fail."

Developing project teams to reach their fullest potential through effective teamwork is an essential leadership skill with many complexities. Team members are likely to be cross-cultural, geographically dispersed or virtual, multi-generational, possessing different backgrounds, skills and experiences, and working internally, externally, or contractually. All of these factors require effective team planning to lead the team to develop to a level of extraordinary performance. Team leaders must understand team dynamics, grasp the concept of shared responsibility and accountability, and foster synergy through effective team planning.

In this unique book *Team Planning for Project Managers and Business Analysts*, Gail Levitt has done excellent work explaining the importance of a systematic process for team planning according to specific performance measurements. Dr. Levitt has provided practical tools and templates that will guide project managers and business analysts in establishing and communicating team operating norms and processes, setting milestones, creating a team vision, and writing a comprehensive team development plan.

This book also offers useful tips and ideas for how to get "real" buy-in for the team development plan from team members and senior management. It emphasizes the importance of developing multi-generational teams that work constructively together, and creating a team succession plan for the benefit of organizational longevity.

The many templates and guidelines presented in *Team Planning for Project Managers and Business Analysts* will help leaders, project managers, and business analysts across all industries gain management's support and command the resources necessary to plan their teams' development to achieve high performance and superior results through effective team collaboration.

Vijay K. Verma, PMI Fellow, PMP, MBA, P.Eng.
Manager, Project Management Services, TRIUMF (Canada's National Research Library located at University of British Columbia)

Author of the following books:

Organizing Projects for Success
Human Resource Skills for the Project Manager
Managing the Project Team

Vancouver, BC, Canada

Introduction

Over the years, project leaders I have trained, coached, and mentored have asked me where they can find templates for a team development plan. Frustrated because they could not find any in their own fields of project management and business analysis, they hoped that I could tell them where to look for some. I was also unsuccessful in my search. So I decided to create some especially for them. After testing and perfecting team development plan templates appropriate for most busy project managers (PMs) and business analysts (BAs), these team leaders encouraged me to make these tools available to a broader base of their professional peers and include other strategic and tactical team planning resources they found useful.

Team Planning for Project Managers and Business Analysts is the result of these efforts. Project professionals seeking practical guidelines, tips, tools, and templates for developing teams will find them in this book. All of the resources apply to diverse teams of two or more people colocated; geographically dispersed or virtual; crosscultural and crossgenerational; formed recently or years before; functional, crossfunctional, or project based; staffed by members working fulltime, parttime, and by contract; and working in offices, on sites, or from home. The contents are designed for use by experienced or inexperienced individuals having full, partial, or no formal authority to lead team members, including project coordinators, project managers, business analysts, team leaders, subject matter experts, sponsors, consultants, vendors, and other project team partners.

Team Planning for Project Managers and Business Analysts focuses on *team planning* as a deliberate, systematic process dedicated to establishing and communicating performance guidelines and milestones for leading the team through the stages of its life cycle. It provides essential knowledge and resources that project professionals need to develop teams successfully. This covers:

- Team Planning as a Mindset
- STARS® Team Assessment Method
- Team Development Plan
- Creating the Team Vision
- Team "SWOT" Analysis

- Getting Buy-In for the Team Development Plan
- Developing Multigenerational Teams
- Facilitating Team Development at Meetings
- Team Succession Plan
- Leading Team Transformation
- The Future of Team Planning

Each chapter begins with a real-life project scenario, highlights essential concepts and tips pertinent to each topic, and ends with a summary of key points. The Appendix contains essential team planning templates created especially for project professionals to enhance their efficiency and effectiveness. Recommended books and websites most appropriate for project professionals to increase their team development skill competencies are listed in the Selected Bibliography at the end of the book.

Effective team planning is a core skill for effective team leadership. I hope this book gives project leaders the support and resources they need to plan their teams' development proactively to achieve performance goals more productively.

Dr. Gail Levitt

About the Author

 **Gail Levitt, Ph.D.,** is a knowledgeable leadership strategist, facilitator, and coach dedicated to developing global leaders and their teams to perform more efficiently and effectively. She provides a unique perspective as a former marketing administrator, business development strategist, product manager, project team leader, and corporate consultant.

Levitt is president of Levitt Communications Inc., a corporate service organization offering courseware, templates and tools, training, and consulting in leadership communications, especially related to team problem solving, conflict management, collaboration, and influence. Previously, she worked for twenty years for leading organizations in publishing, packaged goods, computers, education, and government, resulting in extensive expertise in leadership and team development pitfalls and best practices. She has spoken extensively at conferences on project management, business analysis, customer service, and team development and has written articles on team leadership issues for professional publications. The recipient of numerous awards for poetry, she has also presented academic papers at the *International Conference on the State of Mark Twain Studies* at Elmira College for three consecutive years.

Gail Levitt holds a doctorate in cultural studies from the University of Exeter in England. She also earned a master's degree with high honors in English from the University of Illinois in Urbana-Champagne, and a bachelor's degree in English from Hobart and William Smith Colleges in Geneva, New York, graduating summa cum laude.

1

Team Planning in a Project Environment

George, BA (Business Systems Analyst): *"Hi, Carol. I'm looking forward to your requirements presentation at the project update meeting tomorrow."*

Carol, PMP (Project Team Leader): *"Well, as a matter of fact, I'm not going, but don't worry—you will receive the information you need from Henry who will be presenting instead."*

George: *"O.K., that's acceptable, but why are you going to miss the meeting?"*

Carol: *"The project sponsor is requiring me to attend a 'team planning' course for the next two days. I tried to postpone this training due to my workload, but I was unsuccessful."*

George: *"So while we are completing important project work priorities, you will be having fun doing silly team-building games and learning fluffy, touchy-feely stuff. You are really lucky to have it so easy!"*

Carol: *"I don't feel so lucky wasting my time and energy when I have so much real work to do, but I don't have a choice. I just hope there is a quiet location outside the room where I can disappear frequently to check messages for project updates."*

STEREOTYPE OF TEAM PLANNING

In the above dialogue, George and Carol define *team planning* as a touchy-feely activity identical to *team building* that interferes with more important project tasks. Have you ever heard or participated in a similar conversation that stereotypes team building and development processes as irrelevant, silly, and a waste of time? I certainly have—and not just once—but all too often during my extensive career as a project manager and team developer. The purpose of this chapter is to correct that stereotype by providing relevant information about team building and team planning that project professionals can use proactively to become more productive in the workplace.

There is no easy answer to the question: Why is *team planning* sometimes stereotyped in project management and business analysis as "touchy-feely"? This requires a more detailed analysis to understand how the unique challenges and experiences of project managers and business analysts affect their perceptions of team planning. There are four key contributing factors to consider:

1. *Professional competency.* Project managers and business analysts have specialized training in their respective disciplines that encourages them to follow specific processes. Although they typically work on teams as part of their jobs, their project duties do not require *professional competency* to strategically plan for and develop the team throughout the stages of its life cycle. As the wise writer Mark Twain once commented, "Men are usually competent thinkers along the lines of their specialized training only. Within those limits alone are their opinions and judgments valuable; outside of them they grope and are lost—usually without knowing it."[*] Unless they have seen a team development plan before, there would be no reason for project managers and business analysts to know anything about it.

   In my experience training and coaching approximately 1,200 project managers and business analysts annually, only 20 percent of them have ever seen a team development plan. Paramount to the *professional competency* of team planning is acquiring in-depth knowledge to assess, influence, and evaluate the team's stages of development. Knowing how to write, execute, and evaluate a team plan is an essential skill for project managers and business analysts challenged to develop a team, with or without formal authority over its members.

2. *Intolerance of ambiguity.* In a project environment, the ability to objectively define and precisely document ambiguous information is an essential skill that enables project managers and business analysts

---

[*] Twain, Mark. "Christian Science," *The Works of Mark Twain: What Is Man? And Other Philosophical Writings.* Ed. Paul Baender. Berkley: University of California Press, 1973, p. 260.

to effectively solve problems and make decisions. Refining vague details ensures that the project scope, requirements, evaluation criteria, and deliverables are consistent and clear to all team members and stakeholders. Clarifying vague information can also reduce risks to quality, productivity, and revenue loss. Consequently, poorly defined requirements, scope, and deliverables can be attributed to a project professional's inability to eliminate ambiguity.

Too much emphasis on avoiding ambiguity, however, can lead to serious team performance issues. Team members and their leaders can become so comfortable with predictable routines and processes that their avoidance of risk and change can lead to missed opportunities for quick decision making and innovation. This response, known as *ambiguity intolerance*, occurs when individuals and teams experience high levels of anxiety and stress and low levels of performance while they struggle to cope with information that is vague, imprecise, incomplete, and inconsistent. Their ambiguity intolerance can also cause them to become impatient when others do not provide clear and consistent project information. Consequently, interpersonal tensions and conflicts can emerge among team members, stakeholders, and customers who do not express ideas and requirements in terms that are concrete or tangible.

Ambiguous situations can challenge project professionals to overcome their resistance to change, explore problems and opportunities from new perspectives, and make sounder decisions. Developing a high tolerance for ambiguity can lead to increased innovation, collaboration, and customer responsiveness. Teams capable of addressing ambiguity with confidence have a better chance of developing to their full potential by becoming strengthened by the unforeseen obstacles they overcome together as a consolidated unit.[*]

3. *The triple constraints.* Through no fault of their own, many competent project managers and business analysts still struggle to find ways to cope with the continuous anxiety they feel about managing their everexpanding workloads on their current to-do list. They can feel stuck on the front lines of endless daily tasks, what productivity specialist David Allen refers to as the runway of current actions that seem to constantly

---

[*] Refer to this book for more information about the advantages of ambiguity tolerance: Wilkinson, David J., *The Ambiguity Advantage. What Great Leaders Are Great At.* Houndmills, England: Palgrave MacMillan, 2006.

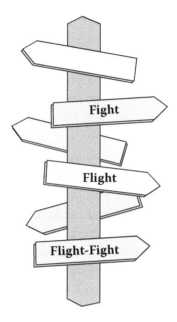

FIGURE 1.1
Conflict reactions signpost.

multiply and never get done.* On the project runway, daily routines and short-term deliverables take priority. The risk is perceiving important activities, including team building and team planning, as an interference with getting things done when both can contribute to increased productivity if sufficient time is allocated for each of them.

4. *Stress and conflict reactions.* The pressures related to these triple constraints can lead to anxiety and feeling a loss of control, which in turn can put busy project managers and business analysts at risk for experiencing increased stress and conflict reactions on the team (Figure 1.1). The adrenaline that triggers one's stress and conflict responses can generate three responses:
   a. Fight
   b. Flight
   c. Flight–Fight (Passive-aggressive)

A "fight" reaction is demonstrated by a forceful, aggressive approach to meeting the stressor or conflict directly. In contrast, a "flight" response is more indirect; it involves wanting to withdraw from the stressors or conflict.

---

* Allen, David. Getting Things Done: The Art of Stress-Free Productivity. Toronto: Penguin Books, 2001, p. 51.

When a "flight" response escalates into a "fight" response, the result is known as a passive-aggressive reaction. Although these three responses occur as a natural part of human interactions, it is possible for project professionals ill-prepared to deal with their own or others' emotions to view them as "touchy-feely" responses that are not appropriate in a project environment.

The reality is that these conflict responses often occur so quickly that by the time they escalate, they become difficult and time-consuming to resolve. Self-control of these responses, individually and collectively, is paramount to the stability and productivity of teams; the role of team planning is to ensure more effective conflict management. The intelligent use of one's emotions to assess, observe, control, adapt, and evaluate is known as "emotional intelligence," or EQ. This is a powerful way to self-manage one's stress and conflict reactions. The more highly developed a team is in its life cycle, the more likely it is that all of its members view conflict as a necessary part of its growth. The team will ensure sufficient group processes are in place to uncover pressing issues and manage conflict proactively.

TRUTH ABOUT TEAM PLANNING

The core of team planning is a formal written document called a *team development plan*. The *team development plan* outlines the objectives, strategies, and tactics for directing and supporting the team through each stage of its life cycle over a specified period of time, and in alignment with the team vision, mission, and goals. The five stages of the team life cycle are forming, storming, norming, performing, and adjourning.*

Effective team planning requires a mindset that is both visionary and methodical. The following highlights the characteristics of each.

Visionary

A visionary mindset sees the true potential of the team in the present and insists on making it the central focus of the team's growth for the future. This mindset resists getting distracted by short-term crises and makes

---

* Tuckman, Bruce W., and Jensen, Mary Ann C. (1977). Stages of small group development revisited, *Group and Organizational Studies*, 2: 419–427.

sound decisions based on how team planning strategies, objectives, and tactics connect to the overall vision for the team. The team vision is its ideal state of thinking, interacting, and performing in the distant future. The team vision can embody many elements, including the team's purpose, values, aims, unique talents, contributions, and preferred image. The team vision is not a date, a budget number, a requirement, or anything else on the busy runway of current activities. It is an essence less tangible but equally powerful; it is what motivates and unifies the team. The team vision should challenge the team sufficiently by being an imagined state of its future achievement as a cohesive unit.

Experienced team planners know the power that this futuristic mindset has to engage all members in a common purpose. Andy Thomas, a project management facilitator with international experience, emphasizes that "project success can only be assured when all team members and key stakeholders have a common goal in view. I ask the team, 'If that's what success looks like, what do we have to do to make it real?'" As champions of the team's successful development, team development planners and leaders need to maintain a consistent mindset that keeps the team vision top of mind as the central focus of the team's identity and actions.*

The team vision should serve as an anchor attached directly to the team's mission, goals, and deliverables, as Figure 1.2 illustrates.

---

* Andy Thomas, PMP, interview, August 31, 2011.

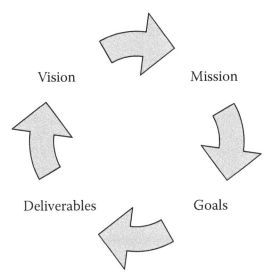

TEAM VISION: A vision communicates a clear picture of a future state that represents success in broad terms.

> **Example:** *To be perceived globally as the team that offers customers a humane approach to learning and using information technology for enhanced work performance.*

TEAM MISSION: A mission is a general statement that identifies the overall approach to achieving the vision.

> **Example:** *For each team member to know and understand our customers' learning styles and working needs.*

TEAM GOALS (Short- to Moderate-term): A goal is a more specific statement that addresses the key objective or result that will help achieve the mission.

> **Example:** *To achieve a minimum score of 4.8 out of 5.0 from customer surveys to evaluate the "humane" attributes of information technology service and support.*

FIGURE 1.2
Team Flow Cycle

TEAM DELIVERABLES (Short-term) (Micro): A deliverable is a certain task or project to be accomplished by a specific date, using specific resources to achieve a specific purpose, and using specific guidelines for measuring and evaluating the results.

> *Example: To complete the information technology pilot survey for Category A customers by next quarter within 90 percent of budget and in accordance with the corporate standards for "humane customer service."*

FIGURE 1.2 (continued)
Team Flow Cycle

Methodical

Demonstrating a methodical mindset is a competency that business analysts already use for process analysis of workflow when they break it down into task sequences, decisions and loops, and parallel processing. As well, when business analysts investigate the root causes of a business problem, they need to methodically identify where the problem is occurring. They can use different models to structure their approach, such as workflow modeling, metrics, process enablers, and data modeling, to check the accuracy of the information required and used by a business process. Project managers apply this same approach using a work breakdown structure (WBS) to identify component parts within each phase of the project planning process. Business analysts need to be equally methodical when preparing a requirements work plan (RWP). These are all examples of establishing a sequential approach for analysis and prioritization.

Team planning requires the same methodical mindset, except that the application is different. Team planning requires special attention to details about specific processes for tasks and approaches to relationships that team members implement to direct and support the team through each stage of its development. This includes a systematic approach for identifying, evaluating, and improving the strengths and gaps in the team's methods to achieve the team's performance objectives. Team development planning is an analytical process for identifying the methods that the team will follow for

- Assigning roles and responsibilities
- Discussing

- Agreeing
- Disagreeing
- Transferring knowledge
- Deciding
- Setting expectations
- Gaining commitment
- Relaxing
- Learning
- Prioritizing
- Publicizing to other teams
- Informing and influencing stakeholders

An essential component of team planning is to assess each of these processes based on specific quantitative and qualitative performance indicators, all of which should be included in the team plan. Some of the quantitative indicators are frequency, consistency, quality, chronology, and accuracy. Examples of qualitative indicators are self-assessments, interviews, and lessons learned. It is likely that some of these indicators will rely on the observation powers of the team developer and input from others interviewed for feedback.

Observant

To be effective, team planners need to have an observant mindset that notices the subtle differences in the ways individuals and teams react in different situations. Knowing what behavioral patterns to watch for and address can be affected, to some, degree by the observer's sensory and intuitive skills. An observant mindset helps the team identify, evaluate, direct, support, and influence the team's behaviors for planned growth. The most important patterns that have a direct impact on the team's ability to progress from one stage to the next are as follows:

- Proxemics–physical distance between individuals on teams
- Vocalics–use of voice and tone in team communications
- Context–two types: "low" prefers written documentation and rules, whereas "high" prefers spontaneity and oral agreements
- Chronemics–attitudes about time: punctuality (monochromic) or intuitive time that flows (polychromic)

- Identity–reference for self-reliance (individualism) or group reliance (collectivism)
- Authority–trust or distrust in authority
- Ambiguity–comfort levels with ambiguous information: high or low tolerance

Each of these indicators can reveal vital information about the team's performance and productivity levels. The more team members are aware of their own individual and collective patterns, the greater their capacity to plan, discuss, implement, and evaluate how they will progress to the next stage of development.

A key responsibility for the team planner is to strategize how the team will reach its full potential. For the team to progress successfully in its life cycle, its members must apply two different kinds of abilities:

Intellectual Intelligence (IQ) for purposes of knowledge transfer to build and apply technical skill proficiencies in project management and business analysis.

Emotional Intelligence (EQ) for purposes of social awareness, self-control of emotions, and resiliency to manage interpersonal differences, overcome obstacles, and change.

The following chart outlines and contrasts the abilities and key focus for IQ and EQ:

IQ—Intellectual Ability

Abilities—How readily new things are learned

- Analytical thinking
- Logical reasoning
- Abstract and conceptual thinking
- Spatial perceptions
- Verbal and mathematical abilities

Focus—The thinking capacity we are born with

- Retaining and recalling objective information
- Reasoning methods and processes
- Calculating and computing numbers
- Problem-solving using acquired knowledge
- Concentrating, planning, and organizing material
- Using words to assimilate and interpret facts
- The quantitative measurement of one's "personal information bank" of memory, vocabulary, and visual-motor coordination

EQ—Emotional Ability

Abilities—What we do with what we learn and experience: how we process it

- Assessing the political and social environment
- Grasping intuitively what others want and need
- Perceiving and interpreting others' strengths and areas for development
- Managing and changing one's situational reactions to stress and conflict
- Self-assessing and regulating one's emotions for resiliency
- Communicating one's needs and concerns assertively and diplomatically in socially appropriate ways
- Perceiving emotions to promote emotional and intellectual growth

Focus—"Social intelligence" that is dynamic

- Handling conflict and stressful situations with emotional maturity
- Being honest and diplomatic with self and others
- Contributing to community awareness
- Adapting to change with resiliency

An effective team planner with an observant mindset maintains neutrality when evaluating IQ and EQ indicators on teams. He or she recognizes that for the team to reach its fullest potential, its members must demonstrate an equal balance of each quotient.

TEAM PLANNING SKILLS

Team planners need to demonstrate proficiency in twelve essential skills to direct and support teams to develop to their maximum potential:

1. Team Development Knowledge: Understanding how to diagnose and develop each stage of the team in its life cycle.
2. Writing Expertise: Knowing how to write a team development plan that includes a team vision statement, objectives, strategies, and tactics for each stage.
3. Performance Appraisal Proficiency: Identifying appropriate quantitative and qualitative performance indicators for individual and team performance, and communicating feedback constructively.
4. Leadership Effectiveness: Applying the strategies and tactics necessary to direct, coach, mentor, and entrust the team at each stage in the team's life cycle.
5. Influencing Power: Gaining buy-in and commitment from the team and all internal and external stakeholders directly or indirectly involved.
6. Conflict Management Expertise: Knowing about the different conflict styles and taking a proactive approach to guide the team in learning how to manage conflicts constructively.
7. Multi-generational Knowledge: Appealing to the needs of each generation on a team: their work habits, values, definitions of success, communication style, perceptions of power, authority, knowledge transfer, and productivity.
8. Inter-cultural Competence: Proficiency in cultural orientations such as time, communication, space, power, competition, negotiation, authority, decision-making, group dynamics and processes.
9. Change Management Expertise: Identifying and managing individual and team responses at each stage of the change process.
10. Communication Clarity: Communicating with clarity and fluency, both verbally and in writing, to the team, sponsors, and stakeholders.
11. Group Problem-Solving Knowledge: Proficiency in group problem-solving methods and techniques that foster team collaboration for innovative solutions.
12. Succession Planning Expertise: Knowledge of succession planning strategies and tactics to ensure the transfer of knowledge and skills within the team throughout its life cycle.

SUMMARY: KEY IDEAS

Team Building vs. Team Planning: Team building activities are tactical elements of the team development plan, primarily to build rapport, trust, and synergy. Team planning requires creating and following a strategic document that identifies performance goals, methods, and measurements to direct and guide the team through its stages of development in its life cycle.

Misconceptions about team planning derive from the following sources:

- Differences in professional competency
- Intolerance of ambiguity
- Triple constraints
- Stress and conflict reactions

Team Planning Mindset: Having a team planning mindset is necessary to be successful as a team planner. There are three dimensions to the mindset:

1. Visionary
2. Methodical
3. Observant

Team Planning Skills: The twelve essential skills for project managers and business analysts to be effective team planners include:

(1) Team development knowledge
(2) Writing expertise
(3) Performance appraisal proficiency
(4) Leadership effectiveness
(5) Influencing power
(6) Conflict management expertise
(7) Multigenerational knowledge
(8) Intercultural competence
(9) Change management expertise
(10) Communication clarity
(11) Group problem-solving knowledge
(12) Succession planning expertise

2

Evaluating the Team

Steve, BA (Tester): *"What did you think of the project update meeting that we attended yesterday, Harriet?"*

Harriet (Database designer): *"It was not very productive."*

Steve: *"I wanted to get approval on my test design, but instead we spent most of our time disagreeing with everyone's methods."*

Harriet: *"I was bored initially, but it got more exciting when Jake stormed out of the room after calling Sue too aggressive, which made Sue cry. Fred continued to ramble on about unimportant details related to your test design model."*

Steve: *"It reminded me of home. I have three teenaged kids, and it felt the same."*

Harriet: *"Yeah, I think it has something to do with the storming stage of team development."*

Steve: *"How did you get to be so smart?"*

Harriet: *"Oh, we learned about it at a leadership course I took last year."*

Steve: *"So how long did they say this is supposed to last?"*

Harriet: *"The leadership expert said this stage can last for years without effective team planning and strong leadership."*

Steve: *"Well, I guess we're in trouble then."*

TEAM LIFE CYCLE

In the opening dialogue, Steve and Harriet console each other about how stressful it is to witness a team's inability to manage disagreements at a project meeting. They criticize their peers for apparently adolescent behaviors that Steve finds similar to those of his teenaged kids. United in their self-appointed superiority, Steve and Harriet blame Jake for being too aggressive, Sue for being too sensitive, Fred for being too obsessive about details, and their leader for being ineffectual.

According to Patsy Bolton, Senior Accredited Counselor with the British Association for Counselling and Psychotherapy, associating team behaviors with family is about expectations as well as associations:

> "When we come into a group, it's like we are coming into our family. What happened there could determine how we believe this group will react. People tend to transfer their expectations of others and project onto them our wishes, hopes, and fears. We do this as a way of coping"[*].

All of these responses, including both Steve's and Harriet's, are defensive conflict reactions from members on a team whose progress beyond its present stage of storming is uncertain. Team progression does not just happen naturally. A team's development depends on more than the project test approvals, requirements, deadlines, and deliverables their members seek to achieve. Although these deliverables are important for projects to be successful, they are the output—not the lifeblood—of teams. Teams mature because of people. Without the commitment of their members, and appropriate leadership direction and support, a team will not be able to progress through its life cycle completely.

The team life cycle is based on a generally accepted group process model by Bruce Tuckman and Mary Ann Jensen[†]. There are five stages in the team life cycle. Each team stage requires a different leadership emphasis on task and relationship behaviors for maximum team performance. Task behaviors are any activities directed toward getting things done. Relationship behaviors are any activities designed to build relationships. Whereas some teams progress through each stage consecutively, other teams may remain in one stage indefinitely, or regress to a previous stage. The chart in Table 2.1 highlights each stage and the relative focus of task and relationship behaviors.

Five Team Stages: Task and Relationship Focus

These five team stages require further review to understand exactly what distinguishing characteristics of each to observe (Table 2.1).

---

[*] Patsy Bolton, Senior Accredited Counsellor, British Association for Counselling and Psychotherapy interview, December 19, 2012.

[†] Tuckman, Bruce W., and Jensen, Mary Ann C. (1977). Stages of small group development revisited, *Group and Organizational Studies*, 2: 419–427.

TABLE 2.1

The Five Team Stages: Task and Relationship Focus

Team Stage	Focus	Leadership Emphasis
Forming	Achieving tasks	Directing individual task completion
Storming	Improving relationships	Coaching individuals on interpersonal relationships and re-focusing the team on performance standards
Norming	Enhancing task processes using relationships	Establishing team processes for completing tasks efficiently and making decisions collaboratively
Performing	Balancing tasks and relationships	Achieving self-reliance for maximum performance and innovation based on trust
Adjourning	Celebrating relationships	Celebrating past accomplishments and managing anxiety about disbanding

Observing Team Strengths and Gaps

Although teams can achieve goals at any stage, the further they progress in their life cycle, the higher their productivity output as a cohesive unit. When a team gains or loses members, the team may regress to one or more previous stages. A team's progress to each stage is not inevitable with time. Strong leadership is required to identify the stage and provide the appropriate direction and support to build team member task and relationship skills. The following descriptions explain the productivity strengths and gaps of each team stage:

Forming (Infancy): The team functions at a basic skill level. Members perform tasks individually based on assigned roles and responsibilities. They participate in limited decision making, usually by consensus to avoid disagreement and conflict. The team strives to be productive by supporting and respecting each member's individual task completion according to time, scope, resource allocation, and quality standards.

Storming (Adolescence): The team struggles with its growing independence. While members begin to express their differing views about work tasks and relationships, tensions can surface easily in the form of gossip, disagreement, and conflicts. The team attempts to complete tasks using individual and collective problem solving, but the distractions of interpersonal issues can interfere considerably with productivity.

Norming (Early Adulthood): The team develops competency and settles into a routine. The team accomplishes this by creating and implementing agreed-upon procedures and processes for mutual problem solving, knowledge transfer, and task completion. Members attempt to be tolerant and supportive of one another's differences. They begin to balance both task and relationship activities to achieve more consistency and efficiency collectively. However, if members become too comfortable with their routines and resist change, they risk the team's productivity decline.

Performing (Middle Age): The team becomes self-reliant and performs consistently at peak productivity levels based on maximum proficiency in task and relationship processes. Members confidently challenge each other and the group's processes and methods to contribute their skills and ideas for the benefit of the team's success. Productivity results from members' commitment to the proficiency and unity of their team. The fast pace of performance sometimes leads to delays in bureaucratic paperwork or documentation.

Adjourning (Retirement): Having reached the performing stage, the team faces some anxiety about disbanding while it also celebrates its successes. Members support each other to overcome anxieties about being separated from the team "family." Members simultaneously celebrate their unity and prepare for their futures on different teams. Team productivity results from professional and personal support to perform final duties interdependently and mourn the end of their team life together. Members' anticipation of leaving and their uncertainty about their future experiences on the next team can detract from task efficiencies.

OBSERVING TEAMS IN CONFLICT

There is nothing more revealing about a team's stage of development than how its members cope with conflict. Each stage presents differing approaches that the team members use individually and collectively to address and resolve the conflict. The extent of the conflict depends not only on the problem or issue involved, but also on the skill of the team in addressing it early before it escalates. Those four levels of conflict that can challenge teams are as follows:

1. *Hidden:* There are unspoken tensions, such as avoidance or non-verbal signs of discomfort, but no words are spoken.
2. *Emerging*: Signs of tension or disagreement become visible to outsiders, including negative comments, visible uneasiness, or dislike.
3. *Active*: Tension or disagreement escalates to physical or emotional outbursts of frustration, hurt, anger, and other forceful reactions that are very evident.

4. *Aftermath*: The impact of the conflict can be felt by individuals directly and indirectly involved. The team begins the recovery process while members individually attempt to overcome the related stress and consequences.

A team that is not skilled in managing its own disagreements is likely to experience all four levels of conflict. In contrast, teams that are proficient in addressing conflict proactively are more likely to prevent it from progressing through all four stages and to resolve the conflict more quickly. As a result, these teams usually experience little, if any, changes in their productivity because they are able to move forward from their past to focus on future performance.

Conflict Levels and the Team Stages

Forming Teams: Hidden and Emerging Conflict

In the forming stage, the over-use of consensus for decision making makes the team vulnerable to hidden conflicts they either repress or fail to recognize if they emerge. Because the team strives to preserve harmony at this "honeymoon" stage anyway, when conflicts do emerge, they tend to be underplayed by leaders and other members as signs of poor teamwork. Because the team is not unified as to how conflicts are addressed, when disagreements do emerge, members often experience uncertainty about how to cope.

Storming Teams: Emerging and Active Conflict

The storming stage of a team's life cycle is when the team is most likely to experience serious productivity issues from emerging and active conflict. During this adolescent period of the team's existence, members strive to satisfy their own individual concerns and tend to vocalize what they do not like or what they disagree with. This can lead to extensive in-fighting, gossiping, criticizing, blaming, and overall tension that typically worsen due to the team's lack of knowledge and experience to control disagreement. When emerging conflicts develop into active conflict situations, team members prefer to rely on their individual survival skills instead of turning to other members for help because there is no group process for effective resolution. Individuals can respond either more aggressively (fight), passively (flight), or with a combination of both flight and fight (passive-aggressive). In this battleground of wounded egos and interpersonal disagreements, members can become their own worst enemies as they feel the frustration from continuous conflicts that the team as a collective unit has no systematic process for handling. When active conflicts do occur, the aftermath can cripple a team because of unresolved issues and increased friction between members.

Norming Teams: Active Conflict and Aftermath

In the norming stage, the team develops systematized processes, including standardized methods for addressing emerging and active conflicts proactively. Team members typically encourage group discussion to address issues and avoid conflict escalation using more efficient problem solving. At this stage, team members tend to view conflict as a necessary outcome of team interaction, rather than as an indication of the team's flaws. Consequently, members are more likely to seek ways to encourage and support each other in finding remedies, even at the risk of the conflict becoming more active.

In direct contrast to the storming stage, the norming team is less likely to experience a major decline in productivity because it has already implemented its own processes to recover quickly from active conflicts without serious damage. A norming team tends to focus more on process improvement in the aftermath of an active conflict than a storming team. Members will attempt to re-focus their efforts on their team roles and responsibilities pertaining to team processes to achieve performance goals despite interpersonal challenges.

Performing and Adjourning Teams: All Four Levels

Performing and adjourning teams have gained the maturity to know how each member reacts based on past conflicts. At this stage in the team's life cycle, conflict is perceived as an opportunity for continuous improvement. Members have demonstrated extensive experience discussing and debating emerging issues; and when active conflicts occur, they quickly confront issues head-on without fear. The way performing and adjourning teams handle the aftermath of conflict is typically their best skill. They have had lots of practice coping with all levels of conflict, from hidden to emerging, active, and aftermath. Their collective history in conflict situations with each other has strengthened the team's resiliency. Conflicts are dealt with as opportunities to voice concerns, challenge each other, foster open communication, increase trust, identify lessons learned, and enhance performance through continuous improvement.

IDENTIFYING TEAM STAGES: ART AND SCIENCE

Determining a team's actual stage of development in its life cycle is challenging for those project managers and business analysts with a low tolerance for ambiguity. The clues are not necessarily evident at first glance and can be contradictory. The process is both art and science. When identifying a team's stage of development, one needs to be especially observant to notice the subtle elements that can easily be overlooked. Experienced team developers know that assessing a team's stage requires a patient, scientific approach that acquires, tests, and evaluates information systematically using observation, research, and experimentation. The STARS® method is a practical way to identify a team's stage of development systematically. This methodology is explained below.

STARS® Method

The STARS® method (Table 2.2) is most effective for observing a variety of team interactions to reveal patterns based on consistencies and inconsistencies. These interactions include daily communications in person

TABLE 2.2

The STARS® Method

Say:	What do members say to each other regarding content, tone, context, medium, and formality level?
Tasks:	What processes and procedures do team members use to assign, prioritize, and complete tasks?
Argue:	To what extent do team members agree, argue, and disagree with each other, and what processes do they use for each?
Relationships:	What types of activities, and at what frequency, do team members participate in to develop relationships, communicate, build trust, and adapt to each other's personalities, work styles, and attitudes?
Self-perception:	To what extent do individuals think of themselves as part of a team and work together to the team's benefit?

and virtually, including meetings, emails, teleconferences, and informal gatherings. The STARS® method should be interpreted as general guidelines only when attempting to identify the team's stage of development. It is important to take careful notes of discussions, including actual words and phrases. Materials from team discussions, such as notes, posted ground rules, and samples of diagrams, charts, pictures, and other visuals, can be very useful when assessing the team's stage of development. The following lists key indicators for each stage of the team life cycle using STARS®:

STARS®

Forming (Orientation)

Say:

- Frequent "I" comments reflecting individual member needs, expectations, and experiences.
- Individual questions and statements that convey uncertainty and anxiety about roles and responsibilities.
- Assertive individuals tend to represent the team's view as "we" when in fact they are communicating their own "I" views based on self-interest, the team does not challenge them.
- Limited self-disclosure among members.
- Members are careful and cautious about what they say.
- There is minimal open discussion about how individual preferences and behaviors impact the group as an entire unit.

Tasks:

- Assigned and completed based on trial and error.
- Members are preoccupied with conducting routine tasks independently.
- Emphasis is on who, what, and when for each individual's workload.
- No formalized group process for collective task completion or knowledge transfer.
- Tendency for uneven distribution of tasks among team members as more conscientious individuals take on more work.
- Minimal time spent debating ideas and testing assumptions because the focus is more on agreement than on effective problem solving.
- Wording among team members is likely to be related to what each one can and cannot do based on individual workloads.

Argue/Agree:
- Over-emphasis on consensus.
- Avoidance of disagreement and controversy.
- Low tolerance for investing time on differing views about approaches to task completion.
- No formal agreement on how the team will argue and agree.
- Assertive members voice their views strongly to influence decisions to their personal advantage.
- Less assertive members and risk-adverse individuals prefer not to challenge the more assertive members.
- Lack of awareness of how one's individual response to pressure affects other members.

Relationships:
- Characterized by a general uncertainty of how to communicate effectively as a unit.
- Individuals attempt to gain support and acceptance from others based on their own styles.
- Low level of awareness of differences in work styles among members.
- There are no formalized processes for enabling each individual to feel emotionally safe and secure from conflict or retaliation.
- More assertive individuals will attempt to advance their own interests over others without asking for consent.
- Nonassertive members will generally avoid responding publicly to avoid conflict or disapproval.
- Trust has not been established within the group as a whole, so there is some anxiety among members that, if not addressed, can lead to cliques and opposing groups in the longer term.

Self-perception:
- Teamwork is viewed as the independent completion of tasks on time, within scope, and on budget.
- There is no agreed-upon identity as a unit.
- The group does not yet have a clear perception of its talents and skill sets.

Storming (Disorientation)
Say:
- "I" language conveying individuals' strong opinions and emotions about others' personalities, roles, responsibilities, competencies, and approaches to completing tasks.

- Heated words of anger, jealousy, frustration, disapproval, defensiveness, and blame toward others on the team.
- Statements that express feeling like the victims of others' mistakes and inadequacies.
- Members say what they feel without the patience and self-control to edit their comments or think about the impact on others.
- "You" language in the blame frame instead of the aim frame for constructive resolution.
- Blaming individual group members or job functions ("management") for being the cause of the team's problems and challenges without taking personal accountability.

Tasks:
- Members prefer to assign some roles and responsibilities based on popularity, perceived power, and politics instead of work-related competencies.
- Individual and collective task completion is reduced due to disagreements about methodologies.
- Members attempt to formalize a team process for assigning and doing tasks despite competing views.
- Members attempt to create a process for knowledge transfer despite losing focus about how others process and apply information differently.

Argue/Agree:
- Individuals blame each other for task and relationship issues.
- Members respond defensively to others' views with conflict reactions of flight or fight.
- Members struggle to create a process for group discussion and problem solving, but it can degenerate easily into personal criticisms and in-fighting.
- Silence exhibited by those who are conflict avoiders can encourage more vocal members to dominate discussions by arguing and attempting to impose their views on the rest of the team.
- Passive-aggressive reactions including eye-rolling, sighs, sarcastic comments, and victimized thinking can interfere with effective team communications and problem solving.

Relationships:
- Characterized by members becoming more aware of individual personality and work style differences and experimenting with new approaches to manage those differences better.

- Direct and indirect defiance and resistance to others who challenge individuals' routine approaches to tasks.
- Individual members form into competing groups or cliques.
- Frequent gossip and rumors, especially about individuals on the team whom others dislike, fear, do not understand, or do not agree with.
- Personality differences contribute to an increase in tension, disagreements, and conflicts between individuals and sub-groups on the team.
- Teamwork exists in sub-groups based on personal and political power plays and alliances, but it is not unified among the entire unit.
- Members feel anxiety and distrust regarding team members who are "different" in style, culture, or work approach and struggle with resultant interpersonal tension and conflict.

Self-perception:
- Teamwork involves dealing with difficult personalities so it is difficult to avoid losing one's focus on the work that each person has to complete.
- The group's growing pains from interpersonal tensions and conflicts create confusion about the team's true identity.
- Members are beginning to discover the talents and skill sets in their group but have not yet figured out how to manage the related power and control issues.

Norming (Standardization)

Say:
- Members develop their own team vocabulary of terms and reference for mutual understanding.
- "I" language to express individual opinions is balanced with "we" and "us" wording to address team needs and priorities.
- The team attempts to spend equal time talking about how they will encourage and support people, what tasks need to be completed, and what processes need to be standardized.
- Members seek to gain each other's commitment by emphasizing mutual team interests, including: customer satisfaction; productivity; fairness; team vision, mission, and values; and solutions to team challenges.

Tasks:
- Task roles and responsibilities are assigned fairly to team members.

- Members settle into a team routine of established procedures and guidelines that they implement consistently.
- Clearly defined processes for knowledge transfer ensure that everyone on the team is informed and trained equally regarding team projects and processes.
- Formalized team processes for improving task quality and efficiency become established.
- Team goals are usually considered a higher priority than each member's own work priorities.
- There are formalized processes for effective knowledge transfer, including coaching and mentoring among team members.
- Members share and delegate tasks to maximize the team's overall performance.
- The team assumes more accountability for initiating, brainstorming, and completing tasks as a unit.
- If members become too comfortable with routine procedures, they can demonstrate resistance to change to the detriment of the team, the organization, and customers.

Argue/Agree:
- Team members follow group norms for self-control in conflict situations to handle disagreements nondefensively.
- The team has established a process for arguing and agreeing that includes ground rules for acceptable and unacceptable behaviors with agreed-upon consequences.
- Members participate in open discussions to share differing viewpoints for the purpose of finding better solutions for the team.
- Members become more proficient at collaborative problem solving based on "us against the problem" as their operating norm for team decision making.
- If members become too accustomed to their own processes and routines, they can lose their tolerance for ambiguity and new ideas.
- The team has processes in place for giving and receiving criticism constructively for purposes of continuous improvement.

Relationships:
- Members begin to tolerate and adapt to each other's styles.
- Members acknowledge and recognize individual and collective achievements.
- Members demonstrate more trust and support toward each other.

- The team becomes more consolidated as a unit with established norms that make it distinct from other teams.
- Members start to learn how to challenge each other to grow instead of criticizing others to fail.

Self-Perceptions:
- Teamwork means focusing on achieving the goal for the team by supporting and encouraging individual efforts.
- The team accomplishes tasks collaboratively by demonstrating assertive and cooperative behaviors most of the time.
- Members understand that a strong team is united by clear processes and different styles, with everyone pursuing the same team vision, mission, and goals.

Performing (Unification)

Say:
- Members say "I," "we," and "us" interchangeably with confidence to convey their unity and self-reliance.
- Individuals communicate with high levels of assertiveness and empathy.
- Members ask team-assessment questions for continuous improvement such as, "How well did we resolve our conflict?" and "What went wrong and how do we improve next time?"
- Individuals converse using their own internal language and references that only they understand within the team.
- Individuals talk frequently with each other to challenge performance goals to achieve as a team.
- Members communicate and take action with a high sense of commitment and urgency about achieving the team vision.

Tasks:
- The team completes tasks with the highest levels of confidence, proficiency, consistency, and dedication.
- Members volunteer for any task required to help achieve team performance goals.
- Members consistently follow established processes for efficient knowledge transfer to others on the team.
- Task roles and responsibilities are assumed interchangeably by all team members at different times to ensure alternates with equal levels of proficiency.

- The team sets and consistently achieves the highest standards for maximum performance.
- Team members challenge themselves and others to do tasks better and differently.
- Members inspire each other to take risks to become more innovative in achieving personal and team goals.

Argue/Agree:

- Team members are comfortable discussing and disagreeing using a principled process that ensures total participation.
- Members have learned how to argue well to challenge each other to apply the best ideas to achieve or exceed team goals.
- The team continuously challenges and changes its own processes for ongoing improvement and development as top performers.
- Members demonstrate effective conflict and stress management skills for team resiliency under pressure.
- Members consider that learning from their mistakes is more important than doing things right.

Relationships:

- Members fully accept and encourage each other to grow despite risks.
- Individuals demonstrate mutual trust and respect in all interactions.
- The team prides itself in being open and honest at all times.
- Team members avoid gossip with sub-groups as they interact candidly and spontaneously with each other to be supportive.

Self-Perception:

- The team is a self-reliant unit comprised of proficient, dedicated, and confident individuals.
- Team members encourage risk-taking and innovation to achieve and exceed performance goals.
- Teamwork means being able to assume many roles and responsibilities to ensure the continuity of the team as a successful unit.
- Team spirit is needed to ensure that being together is a fulfilling learning experience for each member.

Adjourning (Disbanding)

Say:

- Frequent references to the team as "us" and "we."

- Members express sadness and regret about their team having to disband.
- Members share good memories about the team's history.
- Team members express individual anxiety about joining a new team.

Tasks:
- Roles and responsibilities are assigned for efficiency purposes mainly to achieve all team goals and obligations.
- Members finalize documentation for project archiving purposes, including lessons learned.
- Individuals prepare for team activities to celebrate and say good-bye.
- Individuals explore options for their futures on other teams.

Argue/Agree:
- Members share openly how they feel about the team disbanding.
- Members collaborate on lessons learned from their collective team experience that they can apply in the future on new teams.
- Members feel the need to discuss memories about their past team experiences with each other.
- Members try to find meaningful ways to say good-bye to the team.

Relationships:
- Members find it difficult to fully accept that the team is actually disbanding.
- Individuals turn to each other for emotional support and networking advice for future options outside the team.
- Team members feel and express pride for their mutual accomplishments.
- Team members feel the need to reaffirm and celebrate their close ties.

Self-Perception:
- The team is a cohesive family that is about to experience a permanent separation.
- Individuals perceive that they have grown both personally and professionally as a consequence of their membership on the team.
- Members recognize that although the team is disbanding, they will remain emotionally and professionally linked in the future through their memories and collective accomplishments in the past.

SUMMARY: KEY IDEAS

Team Life Cycle

Teams have a life of their own. Although they may not reach all five stages in the life cycle, there is potential for that to happen. At each stage, the team expends time and effort in different ways to complete tasks and develop relationships (see Table 2.3).

Team Stages

At each stage of its development, the team is capable of performing and getting results, but in different ways:

Forming (Infancy): The team functions at a basic skill level.
Storming (Adolescence): The team struggles with its growing independence.
Norming (Early Adulthood): The team develops competency and settles into a routine to complete tasks in a standardized way.
Performing (Middle Age): The team gains its independence to achieve group identity on its path to reach its peak productivity through interdependence and mutual trust.
Adjourning (Retirement): Having already reached the performing stage, the team faces some anxiety about disbanding while it also celebrates its successes.

STARS® Method

Identifying team stages requires creative skills and imagination as well as a scientific approach of systematic observation, data collection, and testing. The STARS® method is a practical and effective method that guides project professionals to know what task and relationship behaviors to observe for assessing the correct team stage of development. Please refer to Table 2.3 as a quick reference guide.

TABLE 2.3

Team Life Cycle

Stage	Description	Focus	Conflict Level
Forming	Needs task direction	Achieving tasks	Hidden and Emerging
Storming	Needs interpersonal coaching	Improving relationships	Emerging and Active
Norming	Needs process improvement	Enhancing task processes using relationships	Active and Aftermath
Performing	Needs to be entrusted	Balancing tasks and relationships	All four
Adjourning	Needs recognition	Celebrating relationships	All four

3

Creating a Team Development Plan

Shauna (Project Sponsor): *"Congratulations on your new assignment to lead the Alpha team."*

Joe (PMP and Team Developer): *"Thanks. You can count on me to get results."*

Shauna: *"Yes, and I am relying on you to develop the team to its full potential. Do you have any ideas about how to do this?"*

Joe: *"Well, a chart outlining roles and responsibilities will be my first priority. If I plan for every team member's role for each project activity, then I am confident that the team will perform well."*

Shauna: *"I agree that defining project roles and responsibilities is a great project delivery tool to determine a team member's key role to be responsible, accountable, and to consult, or inform. Planning these team roles will help you develop the project efficiently. But how are you going to develop the team itself?"*

Joe: *"I can prepare team objectives for the project, establish a team charter, and set team operating ground rules for meetings. That should be sufficient."*

Shauna: *"These are good basic steps for the human resource management of the project, but they are not enough to foster the team's growth throughout its life cycle. Imagine that I was your financial planner and I told you, 'Trust me to manage your monetary resources. I will let you know when it is done.' Would that be enough for you to take me at my word, even if I was the best financial planner in the world?"*

Joe: *"Of course not! I would want to see a plan of action for how the money would be invested, along with profit and loss updates quarterly."*

Shauna: *"Precisely. Developing a team is similar. You need to plan very carefully for how you will invest time and energy to guide the growth of your team so it reaches its maximum potential and you need to do it formally in writing. You have to protect your investment. That is what the team development plan does."*

Joe: *"I can appreciate what you are saying in theory, but in practice it sounds like a lot of work."*

PROTECTING YOUR PROJECT ASSETS

The dialogue above is based on a true situation that occurred between a sponsor and a star project manager in an IT environment in the telecommunications industry. The project manager had been a subject matter expert in IT systems development for five years and was very reliable about performing tasks himself with high-quality results. This individual, or "Joe" as I have named him above, was the first subject matter expert on his team of business analysts and was identified as a high potential leader by the project sponsor in the organization. Joe was a technically competent, task-oriented professional who was diligent in meeting deadlines for projects. These qualities contributed to his promotion to Team Developer. He had no direct reports, and many of the people he was supposed to lead had more authority than he did. His responses to Shauna's questions about his plans for team development confirmed her suspicions that he needed more tools and coaching to be able to handle the demands of the new job.

I interviewed Joe after his meeting with Shauna to identify his responses. He was willing to consider creating a team development plan but due to his high task focus, he did not yet recognize the value of investing time now to plan for the future. His mindset was still that of a subject matter expert who had not yet developed a team leadership attitude. Fortunately for Joe, Shauna offered him a coaching lifeline to give him support to write a leadership development plan and discuss how to implement it effectively during his first few months in the new position. When I informed Joe that Shauna had arranged for me to coach him in team development skills, he was relieved. He admitted that he had never seen a team development plan before and asked me to provide him with a template for one. He was concerned that he did not have enough time to create one due to project deadlines.

I was not at all surprised that Joe was not familiar with a team development plan. In a project environment where team development is often ad hoc without a lot of deliberate planning, this tool is not very common; therefore, template samples are difficult to acquire. Also, the project professionals most likely to know about the components of a team development plan have backgrounds in facilitating team development or strategic human resource development. One human resources manager I interviewed indicated that even in her field, team development plans were less common than personal development plans in her experience.

Writing a team development plan takes less time than Joe and other busy project leaders might expect. Once it is completed, a team development plan helps a leader avoid unnecessary team conflicts, crises, personality issues, and time lost as a result. Understanding the components of a team development plan and seeing a visual outline is usually what is needed to motivate project team leaders to complete it without reservation. The remainder of this chapter outlines these components for efficient application. There is also a team development plan template in the Appendix that is "Joe-approved" as "Joe" actually had the opportunity to edit the template and use it successfully for his new leadership activities.

TEAM DEVELOPMENT PLAN: WHAT IS IT?

The team development plan is a baseline document that identifies the team's current stage of development and provides an action plan for guiding and managing its continued growth. The plan outlines the objectives, strategies, and tactics for directing and supporting the team through each stage of its life cycle. This comprehensive document identifies both the quantitative and qualitative measurements for assessing team performance at each stage of its development. It also itemizes the tools, methods, and activities that will be implemented to achieve the specific performance deliverables for each stage and for the purpose of corrective action.

There are many important reasons for creating a team development plan. First, it establishes that all team members are connected to a common purpose that fosters their commitment to become more productive as an interdependent unit. Second, the team development plan serves as a directional map for evaluating progress throughout the team's stages of development in its life cycle. It functions as a guide for charting the deliberate course of action for individual and team development on four levels: vision, mission, goals, and deliverables. Third, it sets quality standards and performance indicators for observing, measuring, monitoring, and evaluating individual and team behaviors fairly and consistently. Finally, the team development plan presents a proactive and productive process for anticipating and tracking progress toward achieving performance goals. It also provides a framework for introducing new members seamlessly into the team.

Team Development Plan Components

A team development plan has four components:

1. Team assessment: stage, behaviors, strengths, areas for development
2. Objectives and strategies: past, present, future
3. Tactics for implementation: for each stage
4. Measurements for success: feedback and refinement

The questions that a team development plan addresses are similar to those for a marketing plan for a product or service. A marketing plan focuses on how to promote a product or service by addressing four key questions:

1. Where was it before?
2. Where is it now?
3. Where is it going?
4. How does it get there?

The team development plan answers these same questions, except that its "product" is the team itself. The purpose of the plan is to direct and support the team to do one of the following:

- Become more effective in its current stage of development
- Reach the next stage(s) of development
- Recover from regression to a previous stage of development

The team development plan document consists of seven key components that are be integrated equally to serve as a guide for observing, developing, and refining the team. These seven components are as follows:

1. Team vision (also identified by the project sponsor in Team Charter document)
2. Team mission (also identified by the project sponsor in Team Charter document)
3. Team goal(s)
4. Team deliverable(s)
5. Team "SWOT" analysis: strengths, weaknesses, opportunities, threats
6. Performance indicators for each stage of team development:
   - Allocation of roles and responsibilities
   - Task focus
   - Relationship focus
   - Tolerance for ambiguity
   - Problem-solving approaches
   - Conflict responses
   - Attitudes about change
7. Performance action plan for each stage of team development:
   - Task competencies
   - Relationship competencies

Each of these components is explained in more detail below.

Team Vision

The *team vision* is the glue that keeps the team together throughout its life cycle. In a busy project environment, team members can easily become self-absorbed with their own tasks and goals and lose sight of how their actions impact the team. Knowing the team vision reminds each team member of his or her connection to something bigger than oneself. The team vision is the reason why the team exists in the first place. It paints the big picture about where the team is going over time. It is an ideal state of existence separate from the restrictions of resources, budget, and scope.

The team vision puts all the smaller realities of deliverables and goals into proper perspective. It communicates a clear picture of a future state that represents success in broad terms. Because the team vision statement focuses on an ideal state long term, it does not typically contain specific references to budget, resources, or deadlines. Those more short-term details are contained in goal and deliverable statements for the team development plan. Table 3.1 shows these four levels in relation to each other.

TABLE 3.1

Team Vision and Supporting Levels

A vision communicates a clear picture of a future state that represents success in broad terms.

> *Example: To be known as the team that demonstrates the three C's consistently: competent, committed, and customer oriented.*

Team Mission

A mission is a general statement that identifies the overall approach to achieving the vision.

> *Example: To ensure that each team member shares knowledge about XYZ Company standards and processes, inspires others to achieve the vision, and demonstrates superior customer service internally and externally to the team.*

Team Goal

A goal is a more specific statement that addresses the key aim or result that will help achieve the mission.

> *Example: Members will be committed to helping each other perform quality work and provide superb customer service ratings so the team will earn consistent customer satisfaction ratings at a minimum level annually of 89 percent.*

Team Deliverable(s)

Once the goal has been identified, the "deliverables" will be determined, which include action steps to achieve the goal based on timelines, scope, and resources.

> *Example: To fulfill individual and collective commitments to complete Project X on time, within budget, within scope, and according to the quality standards identified in the customer agreement.*

Stating the Team's Vision

A team vision statement represents the transformation from "what is" in the present to "what can be" in the future, preferably in at least three years. It is an ideal state to aim for, a future beyond the everyday routines of projects that require a clear focus on the triple constraints of time, scope, and resources. A team vision statement should answer one or more of the following questions about the team's future state:

Team Vision Questions

- Why does the team exist—for what long-term strategy and purpose?
- Why does the team's struggle matter?
- What impact will the team have on: the stakeholders, the organization, other teams, the industry, customers, and one's families?
- What does the team want to be known for longer-term?
- How does the team want others to perceive its image and reputation?
- What does a "successful" team look like?
- What are the team's core values?
- What contribution will the team be remembered for?
- What unique industry standard or market niche will the team achieve?
- What legacy will the team leave behind in the organization or industry?
- What makes the team unique?
- What will the team achieve that is innovative?
- What actions, capabilities, and results will give the team recognition and respect from others?
- What characteristics of the team will distinguish it from all other teams?
- Aside from projects, what will the team accomplish that is of value?
- How will the team affect or change others' lives?
- As a team, what will it become when it "grows up"?

The team vision should be consistent with the project sponsor's expectations, usually included in the team charter, which is part of the document called the Project Plan.

Team Vision Examples

The process of creating a team vision involves strategic, analytical, and innovative thinking. The team vision should be aligned strategically to the long-term vision for the organization based on its business plan. The analytical nature of the team vision answers the key question, "Why will we be successful as a unit in the future?" The innovative elements of the team vision enable it to use analogies, metaphors, comparisons, or other creative wording to illustrate key concepts, principles, or future states of existence. Team vision statements are varied in content and scope. The following are some real-life examples in project management and business analysis that illustrate a wide range of approaches:

Vision statement examples include

- To excel as the most knowledgeable, trusted, and creative project team in the organization.
- To be known as the team that every business analyst wants to join because of its synergy, diversity, and competency in the IT industry.
- We will educate and inspire our stakeholders to achieve change both personally and professionally through our wisdom and innovation in project management.
- To function efficiently and effectively as the "glue" that helps project managers and their customers "stick" together.
- Our team vision is to provide a simple and personalized approach to business analysis that makes a lasting impression on our clients.
- To become respected globally as an industry leader in software development and implementation, creating unique solutions for our stakeholders, employees, and customers.
- To challenge ourselves and our clients to set new standards for quality and innovation in telecommunications.

Determining the Team Mission

The mission identifies the team's overall approach and key focus for achieving its vision. Typically, the team mission is a general statement without specific references to time, money, or resources. The mission should unify all team members in a purpose beyond achieving short-term goals and deliverables. It often accompanies the vision statement in the team charter. The following is an example of a team mission statement that supports the vision:

Team vision: "To be known as the most creative minds in the toy industry."

Team mission: "To ensure that all toy product launches are as creative as the toys they represent."

Setting Team Goals

In a project environment, the key aim or result that team members dedicate themselves to achieving is the team goal. Although it can include references to one or many project goals, the *team* goal is different because it emphasizes more than project outcomes—it stipulates how the team will interact as a cohesive unit to achieve its mission. The following examples show the difference between a project goal and a team goal:

> *Team goal:* "To collaborate on ways to ensure the most innovative software solutions for customers using Software Product XYZ."
>
> *Project goal:* "To launch software product XYZ on time, within budget, and within the scope of specified customer requirements."

Identifying Team Deliverables

Team deliverables are the first level of the project runway. They are usually "SMART": Specific, Measurable, Achievable, Realistic, and Time-activated. An example of a team deliverable is:

> "To launch software Product XYZ to Fortune 500 companies by the fourth quarter within a budget of $500,000 and with a maximum error ratio of 1%."

Team "SWOT" Analysis

A "SWOT" analysis is a fundamental part of the marketing plan for a product or service that provides essential information to address problem solving and opportunity analysis. The acronym "SWOT" stands for Strengths, Weaknesses, Opportunities, and Threats.

As a component of a team development plan, the "SWOT" analysis is a useful tool for project managers and business analysts to include in the project plan because it reveals a team's capabilities and developmental areas along with potential opportunities and obstacles for its future development. It examines the core attributes of that product or service, along with its drawbacks, in comparison and contrast to its competitors.

As well, a "SWOT" analysis identifies potential opportunities and threats to success based on external factors including customer trends, changing economic conditions, and competitive developments. At a glance, the

TABLE 3.2

SWOT Chart Table

Strengths:	What are the team's internal levels of functionality as a unit, especially work knowledge, team processes and procedures, ability to perform tasks accurately and efficiently, and member interrelationships?
Weaknesses:	What are the team's internal areas for development, particularly related to performance, relationships, conflict and stress management, and decision making and problem solving?
Opportunities:	What external factors can help the team grow, including physical proximity; new roles, projects, or tasks; special events; changes to market conditions or technology, global economy, and customer or user trends?
Threats:	What external factors can potentially harm the team's growth and development, especially related to physical proximity; changes to the organization, technology, client and customer trends, market conditions, and economics?

"SWOT" analysis takes a snapshot of the team's status from a developmental perspective by highlighting the ideas shown in the table.

Table 3.2 is an example of a "SWOT" table that appeared in a team development plan. The context is that it was written concerning twenty project managers and business analysts to summarize their current team status working together virtually in three different cities globally.

Performance Indicators

How does one determine the team's current stage of development and decide what skills and behaviors to focus on to guide the team to the next stage? The most effective and efficient way to accomplish this is by identifying team "performance indicators" that are observed and evaluated continuously to compare actual results to predicted improvements that the leader expects over time. These indicators address both task and relationship behaviors within the team as well as interactions with new members, non-members, and other teams in each stage of the team's development.

Each team development plan includes a unique set of performance indicators for observing and planning the team's growth throughout its life cycle. The most common ones are identified and described below based on the four stages of forming, storming, norming, and performing. Every performance indicator is explained based on the general tendencies for each of the team stages.

Team performance indicators include

- *Allocation of roles and responsibilities*: This is the process the team uses to assign roles and responsibilities for tasks. Forming teams will usually base this on job descriptions or volunteers willing to do the tasks. In storming teams, allocation is more likely to be based on popularity, politics, dominant behaviors, or fear of reprisals. In norming teams, the team is most likely to assign roles and responsibilities according to professional and technical competencies and established protocols. In contrast, performing teams typically prefer to assign important roles and responsibilities to members needing to develop more proficiency.
- *Task focus:* The types of tasks that the team prefers are very revealing about its stage of development. Teams in the forming stage emphasize the tactical completion of tasks by each member independently. Storming teams have difficulty staying focused on the task because they are preoccupied with interpersonal tensions and conflicts. Consequently, there are often gaps and inconsistencies in individual and team performance. Teams that have normed tend to focus on tasks that support internal procedures and bureaucracies with an emphasis on conforming to standards consistently and efficiently. Performing teams are more prone to take risks to try innovative approaches to reach the next level of proficiency as a unit.
- *Relationship focus:* The way that team members relate to each other tells a great deal about the team's growth stage. Forming teams work hard to avoid conflict and over-use consensus. Storming teams experience cliques and sub-groups that are adversarial, each one seeking dominance over the other. Norming teams have settled into their relationships by learning how to adapt to differing styles to build member partnerships. Performing teams are more candid and open about giving positive and negative feedback because of their strengthened relationships with each other that were gained from previous tensions and struggles in prior team stages.
- *Tolerance for ambiguity*: The ability to tolerate ambiguity, and even embrace it as a way to build one's own structures and take risks, is the sign of a more mature team. Forming teams tend to be very uncomfortable with ambiguity because of their over-reliance on clarity to complete tasks. Storming teams tend to have the lowest tolerance for ambiguity because their preference for clarity compensates for their

lack of task focus as they struggle with interpersonal tensions and disagreements. Norming teams strive to reduce ambiguity to enable them to conform to established routines and processes. Creating opportunities for norming teams to learn how to develop competency and confidence managing ambiguous information can help them grow to the next stage without being stuck in their own routines for too long. Performing teams thrive on ambiguity because it offers them the chance to take charge independently based on their own assumptions, interpretations, and creative solutions.

- *Problem-solving approaches*: The method that a team uses to solve problems is one of the most important determining factors in identifying its actual stage of development. Forming and storming teams tend to solve problems based on trial and error because members need the time to explore options until they are ready to establish and follow routines and processes. Forming teams over-use consensus because of their conflict avoidance. As a result, the quality of their solutions tends to lack depth and innovation. Members of storming teams tend to assert their individual approaches to solving problems because the team does not know how to manage disagreement yet. At this stage, the team is prone to adversarial reactions and interpersonal rifts because there are no established norms yet for collective problem solving.

  If a team reaches the norming stage, it will generally succeed at ensuring that all members give input. This, in turn, increases the likelihood that the solutions integrate a wider variety of thinking styles and approaches. Performing teams tend to encourage differing viewpoints and disagreement when problem solving. Their capacity to deal with conflicting views enables them to construct innovative solutions that address the problem with more breadth and depth than teams at previous stages of development.

- *Conflict responses*: Forming teams avoid conflict at all costs, preferring consensus over disagreement. When individuals claim to speak on behalf of other team members, they are actually advocating their own personal agendas. These dominant team members are not likely to be challenged publicly at team meetings. However, when asked for anonymous feedback or in personal interviews, many group members will feel more comfortable expressing their own views and differing opinions.

Storming teams tend to exhibit more extreme conflict style ranges of overt aggression, quiet withdrawal, accommodation, compromise, and passive-aggressive reactions. These are all defensive ways of dealing with the team's inability to manage its own differences. Consequently, conflicts related to personalities, opinions, work styles, decisions, and actions from other team members are exaggerated and magnified.

Norming teams apply processes to manage conflicts and unnecessary escalation upward to senior management. Therefore, they can experience the same vulnerability to unmanaged conflict as forming and storming teams. As they settle into standardized work routines and group processes for discussing, disagreeing, and deciding, norming team members are able to handle conflict with minimal disruption to their productivity. If the team reaches the performing stage, then it has become more mature in its treatment of differences and can handle conflict more proactively.

- *Attitudes about change*: The team life cycle involves significant ups and downs until change is accepted as something positive and necessary. Members of forming teams use trial and error to learn more about each other. Members of storming teams can struggle to find their individual voices while feeling overwhelmed by interpersonal tensions and conflicts that are often symptoms of the group's resistance to change. Whereas norming teams initially make changes in their processes to become more efficient as a unit to achieve project deliverables, they can risk being especially resistant to change if they settle too comfortably into routines for too long.

  Performing teams will challenge the status quo in organizations. At times, they will actually try to break the rules to bring about change. Ironically, team members can become so comfortable interacting with each other to play the role of change agents that they can become easily discouraged when trying to influence more change-resistant individuals on teams outside their immediate circle of influence.

Team Performance Action Plan

In a results-driven workplace, "team performance" can be identified superficially to mean completing projects on time, within scope, within budget, and according to specified standards. From the experienced perspective of a team developer, however, "team performance" means much more than team deliverables. Teams can "perform" at each stage of their development, but their processes and outcomes are very different for each stage. The more a team leader understands the strengths and drawbacks of a team's developmental stage, the greater the possibilities for accomplishments at each level.

The value of the team performance section of the team development plan is that it can assist the team leader in assessing the team's current level of performance based on how it manages both tasks and relationships. It also helps the team leader identify exactly what to focus time and energy on to help the team become most productive, regardless of its stage in the developmental life cycle.

For sponsors and leaders who have formal authority over their direct reports, the performance action plan can be very helpful to supplement other performance-related benchmarks, including the job evaluation and work performance review process. For the many project managers and business analysts accountable for leading teams without formal authority, the team performance section of the team development plan functions as more than just a useful resource; it serves as an essential tool for establishing realistic expectations for team performance goals.

The performance action plan addresses how the leader will develop task and relationship competencies during each stage of the team's development throughout its life cycle. Both of these components are explained below.

Task Competencies

Thoroughly assessing the team's collective task competencies is necessary to set reasonable expectations about what the team can realistically achieve presently and in the future as a unit. The key purpose is to identify essential resources, tools, technology, and knowledge that all members need to access and know in order to achieve team performance goals. Determining the team's task competencies also helps to identify gaps in individual task competencies requiring improvement so that the team's performance as a whole will not be shortchanged.

Careful planning is necessary to identify, evaluate, and develop task competencies for the team to achieve in each stage of its life cycle. When creating an action plan for a team to develop its task competencies, one should consider the extent that the entire team has knowledge, dedication, and assuredness based on the following proficiencies:

- The team's knowledge is its collective wisdom to perform tasks correctly and competently. This includes anticipating and planning for knowledge development and transfer within the team so that it can handle task assignments smoothly despite staff attrition.
- The team's dedication is its collective commitment to follow through on task assignments with reliability, responsibility, and accountability.
- The team's assuredness is its confidence to complete those tasks in a satisfactory manner.

The following discussion provides general guidelines for each of these areas. They also feature practical suggestions for specific action steps to implement to determine and develop a team's task competencies for each stage of its life cycle:

Forming: Whether a team is in the forming stage for one year or a decade, the tendencies are still the same: individual members are more self-involved in their own tasks than concerned about how their competencies impact the growth and productivity of the team. Without external intervention, many team members would not initiate updating others about their tasks, preferring instead to complete the work themselves. Consequently, the leader should focus on conducting regular team updates in writing, in person, and virtually to establish a general team habit of information sharing. Additional action items to help team members generate a team knowledge base are as follows:

- Pair two team members with different work styles who do not ordinarily interact on projects to exchange task information and complete all or part of a task together.
- Develop a team website or central database for knowledge sharing for all team members to contribute to and utilize for projects.
- At team meetings, allocate a short segment each time for specific members to share task knowledge and skills on a rotating basis.
- Generate a definition list of key terminology and acronyms related to project tasks that will foster common team language related to task knowledge and resources for all members to access. Post this list on an internal website to use for team projects and recommend its use for new members to access.

Storming: On storming teams, productivity can decline due to interpersonal differences in work style and approaches as well as personality. Team members need both clear direction and empathetic support from their leader to acknowledge and tolerate differing levels of knowledge and task approaches. The following steps are recommended to accomplish both of these results:

- Identify specific guidelines for evaluating individual and team performance effectiveness.
- Review the criteria individually and collectively with team members.
- Coach individual team members on ways to communicate and complete tasks more efficiently and effectively.

Norming: Action planning for the norming stage should include steps to challenge members to become more responsible and accountable for team processes that improve the quality and efficiency of team tasks overall. Collaborative decision making should be the focus of team discussions to fully explore options and resolve business and technical problems thoroughly and efficiently. The following action planning guidelines are recommended:

- Encourage peer reviews of tasks and projects for knowledge sharing and collaboration.
- Introduce new team task methodologies and processes at team meetings that improve collective knowledge and productivity.
- Initiate regular team training sessions and invite special guests for team knowledge development and sharing.
- Engage the team in creating knowledge transfer documentation, processes, and resources for consistency and efficiency.

Performing: Action planning for performing teams should consider that by this stage, members are most concerned about three aspects of task management: task efficiency, succession planning, and lessons learned. The following action planning guidelines are recommended:

- For purposes of succession planning for the team, assign tasks to those individuals requiring more proficiency than the others so the team competency level is distributed equally for proactive responses to emergency situations.
- At team meetings, emphasize individual and collective lessons learned to provide sufficient challenge and self-reliance for team members to be proactive for the future.

- Assign tasks to team members based on a combination of high levels of proficiency vital to the team's image, resiliency, productivity, and overall performance.
- Encourage the team to challenge their task methods and replace them with creative new approaches for testing and experimentation to stimulate innovation.
- Rotate tasks regularly to develop team member task competency and versatility for the sake of the team's overall performance effectiveness.

In addition to task competencies, the team development plan must take into account the relationship competencies the team demonstrates and needs to develop. The following discussion identifies guidelines for effective action planning during its life cycle.

Relationship Competencies

Creating an action plan for deliberately directing and guiding the team's interpersonal competencies over time is essential for ensuring peak performance. Task-oriented project managers and business analysts can sometimes find it difficult to know what action to take because relationship competencies are relatively more challenging to define. The approaches that team members use for interpersonal communications vary from more informal and accidental in the forming stage to habitual and systematic by the performing stage.

Distractions from personality or work style differences, unresolved tensions and conflicts, and miscommunications can cause teams to experience decreases in work productivity that can escalate over time to become difficult to manage, if not impossible to resolve. Teams can also suffer from insulated thinking and poor problem solving due to ineffective group relationship processes. Their ability to manage interactions in nondefensive, productive, and constructive ways is a key indicator of its stage of development.

The team's relationship competencies can be identified accurately using one's powers of observation effectively. The essential relationship competencies are demonstrated by the specific processes the team uses for the following activities according to "The 4 D's" (Table 3.3).

Building a team's relationship competencies requires clear action planning that incorporates all these activities in various ways, depending on the team's stage of development. Team development guidelines for planning and implementation are detailed below according to the team's stage of maturity in its life cycle.

TABLE 3.3

The 4 D's

1	*Discussing:*	What procedures and methods are created, implemented, and enforced to engage members in discussions? What levels of trust are achieved as a result?
2	*Debating:*	To what extent can the members "debate" and disagree about different viewpoints honestly and openly without creating unnecessary tension and conflict? What levels of trust are evident?
3	*Deciding:*	How does the team ensure that its decisions are a true representation of the team in total and not just the desire of a few assertive or dominant individuals in particular?
4	*Debriefing:*	How does the team conduct lessons-learned follow-up to improve internal relationships, build synergy, and increase trust for enhanced teamwork?

Forming: The best way for forming teams to build relationship competencies is by meeting frequently in person or virtually to gain experience by trial and error. Because the team does not yet have a process for discussing, debating, disagreeing, and deciding, it is recommended that simple ground rules of behavior at the meetings be posted, communicated, and enforced to help the team gain experience and confidence. Meetings should include brief and frequent opportunities for team discussions, debates, and decision making regarding a series of simple, low-risk topics or projects. Additional suggestions for action planning to develop relationship competencies in a forming team are as follows:

- Allocate from 10 percent to 20 percent of the time at virtual or in-person team meetings for members to meet and greet each other and learn about their interests, either in pairs, small sub-groups, or round-table introductions.
- Standardize the steps for discussing, debating, disagreeing, and deciding so they become common practice at all group meetings. These steps can easily be incorporated into the agenda and ground rules so the team becomes accustomed to doing them consistently.
- Provide frequent opportunities for members to openly discuss and make small decisions such as: order and sequence of minute items; what times to take breaks; the top three best ideas; the two biggest challenges to discuss. Because the team does not yet know how to decide, learning how to discuss the small things based on decision-making guidelines will prepare them for more difficult and complex topics later.

- Use brainstorming methods to engage individual members in sharing their views publicly.

Storming: Teams that experience the greatest struggle in relationship competencies are typically in the storming stage. Although this struggle is a natural step in its development, without suitable leadership direction and support, a storming team can stay stuck in this stage for a long time, even decades. Careful action planning can help members develop the competencies necessary for enhancing their relationship proficiency individually and collectively, so that the team can progress to its next level of maturity. The most important relationship competency for storming team members is to help them learn how to communicate their views assertively yet diplomatically to each other without resorting to a "fight" or "flight" conflict reaction that is defensive and counterproductive. The following action planning guidelines can be most beneficial for this process to occur:

- Publicize ground rules at all meetings and invite members to add positive words and phrases to use as group norms.
- Regularly assign topics for the team to discuss and debate, and provide constructive feedback on their interpersonal effectiveness, with the assistance of skilled outside facilitators, if necessary.
- Conduct interpersonal coaching for members individually and collectively to develop assertive and diplomatic communication skills.
- Create a website and database for access to team guidelines for appropriate norms for discussing, debating, disagreeing, and deciding.

Norming: Norming team members need to recognize the importance of their interdependence as a unit responsible and accountable for each other. As they become more efficient as a synergistic unit, members need to concentrate more on how they support their colleagues to achieve the overall team vision and mission than on their individual needs. Action planning should emphasize opportunities for active collaboration in problem solving and decision making. The following are guidelines for maximum effectiveness:

- Assign members to lead segments of team meetings on a rotating basis to increase participation levels and showcase diverse work styles.

- Invite members to improve group processes by brainstorming and deciding on small improvements.
- Initiate peer-mentoring processes to encourage interpersonal flexibility and collaboration.
- Assign members to talk about, debate, disagree, decide, and debrief regarding tasks and projects to increase team trust and synergy.

Performing: Performing teams are generally tolerant of the membership diversity, so they thrive on challenging assignments to collaborate with others that have differing skills, perspectives, and needs. The relationship issues needing most development at this stage are ensuring that "honest" feedback is not too blunt or aggressive, and remembering to balance it with responsive emotional support. Action planning for a performing team should emphasize activities that enable members to balance honesty with empathy to build their trust in each other. Action planning guidelines for improving these relationship issues include

- Offering constructive feedback from the leader and team peers on individual and collective communications based on specific guidelines for success.
- Challenging the team to invent new ways to improve their working relationships with each other.
- Assigning a team member at each meeting to be the "leader" and receive constructive feedback about improvements from peers.
- Assigning the team to create a plan of action to improve relationship competencies, and encourage innovative approaches.

SUMMARY: KEY IDEAS

Team Development Plan

The team development plan is an essential resource for leading and developing teams through their life cycles. Although there is no guarantee that teams will ever complete the cycle, writing and implementing a team development plan will create more opportunities for progress and productivity. This plan serves as a baseline document that identifies the team's current stage of development and provides an action plan for guiding and managing the team's continued growth. The purpose of a team development plan is to

- Identify the quantitative and qualitative measurements for assessing team performance at each stage of its development.
- Itemize the tools, methods, and activities that will be implemented to achieve performance deliverables for each stage in the team's life cycle.
- Establish how to communicate and reinforce a vision for the team to follow.
- Present an efficient approach to developing teams that is more proactive than reactive.

The team development plan has four key components:

1. Team assessment
2. Team objectives and strategies
3. Team tactics for implementation
4. Team measurements for success

There are seven sections in the team development plan as follows:

1. Team vision
2. Team mission
3. Team goal(s)
4. Team deliverable(s)
5. Team "SWOT" analysis: strengths, weaknesses, opportunities, threats
6. Team performance indicators
7. Team action plan designating how to develop task and relationship competencies throughout the team's life cycle

4

Getting Buy-In for the Team Development Plan

Josh (Manager, IT Department): *"Now that I have drafted a team development plan, I am concerned that my work has just started. How am I going to sell this to senior management, including the project sponsor?"*

Anna (Manager, Marketing Department): *"Josh, you surprise me by asking for my advice about selling. I know a few IT managers who describe selling as a manipulative process that only slick, money-hungry people resort to when they are desperate! I'm impressed!"*

Josh: *"I am just a realist, Anna. I cannot implement this plan without the buy-in of those people I depend on to support it. Because you have a proven track record for persuading people in authority to do what you recommend, I am counting on you for constructive advice."*

Anna: *"You can rely on me, Josh. What is your influencing goal?"*

Josh: *"I want senior management to understand why it is important to the IT department to invest in team development."*

Anna: *"Interesting. Your goal is more informational than persuasive. It focuses on what's in it for you and your department. Suppose you modify the goal to be more influential by addressing what's in it for the sponsor?"*

Josh: *"All I can think of right now are the IT benefits for our department and customers."*

Anna: *"Just imagine that you are the sponsor. What would really capture your interest as a selling point?"*

Josh: *"I'm not sure."*

Anna: *"Now that's a good start! Not knowing yet means you have an open mind. To be persuasive, you need a mindset that anticipates the interests of your target audience in terms of de-motivators and motivators. This involves thinking carefully about why the sponsor would say 'No', as well as 'Yes.'"*

Josh: *"Will this take a lot of time?"*

Anna: *"I can show you a process that is actually quite efficient once you have mastered it."*

Josh: *"Can I practice on you?"*

Anna: *"Sure. You can also practice on your staff."*

Josh: *"OK. As long as they don't discover some of my new secrets for influencing me to say 'Yes', then I'm willing to give it a try."*

"SELLING" THE TEAM DEVELOPMENT PLAN: CHALLENGES AND OPPORTUNITIES

In the above dialogue, Josh recognizes that preparation to "sell" the team development plan effectively is worth the time and effort. He emphasizes to Anna that the project team will not benefit from the full effects of the team development plan unless sponsors and senior management do more than approve it and invest money for its execution. They also need to endorse, support, and reinforce its strategies, performance evaluation criteria, communications messages, and related work priorities. Otherwise, Josh's lack of support from his management could potentially undermine his success championing the team development plan.

Some business analysts, IT professionals, and subject matter experts might consider "selling" a team development plan to individuals with more power and authority a harder challenge than creating one. Just the thought of having to convince sponsors and senior management to provide appropriate support for team development can cause project managers and business analysts some anxiety, especially if they have not yet developed confidence or fluency in "selling" upward. Before they attempt to influence upward, project professionals need determination to overcome some external and internal obstacles by having an action plan to address them.

External Obstacles

The external obstacles that project managers and business analysts can face when seeking the buy-in and commitment of sponsors and senior managers include

- Politics: Wanting to avoid retaliation or backlash from those with more formal or legitimate power.
- Resources: Competing for limited support such as budget, technology, and staffing.
- Accessibility: Experiencing limited or restricted access to sponsors and senior managers due to virtual locations and travel restrictions.
- Expectations: Coping with others' unrealistic expectations regarding performance outcomes from the team development plan.
- Time: Having limited time to prepare the team development plan presentation.

Internal Obstacles

Whereas these external obstacles are real threats, project managers and business analysts cannot overcome them without mastering their own internal obstacles. Five key internal obstacles pose the greatest challenge to project managers and business analysts seeking buy-in and commitment for the team development plan. These obstacles include

- Fear: Dreading conflict, rejection, disapproval, or failure.
- Lack of self-confidence: Not believing in one's own ability to be persuasive.
- Low self-esteem: Downgrading one's own personal and professional powers.
- Mindset: Perceiving "selling" negatively as manipulation.
- Lack of self-discipline: Neglecting to make time for continuous practice for increased proficiency.

In a project environment, conquering as many of these internal obstacles as possible forms the foundation for overcoming external obstacles with more confidence and focus. Fortunately, influencing upward is easier than many project managers and business analysts expect. The secret is using a deliberate, systematic process that one practices continuously to achieve confidence and fluency. Being accountable for one's own fears, having a positive mindset, and applying self-discipline can lead to success. Being accountable for one's fears, having a positive mindset, and practicing beforehand using a systematic process to gain buy-in and commitment can also pave the way to success.

GAINING BUY-IN AND COMMITMENT: THE PROCESS

To successfully gain buy-in and commitment for the team development plan, it is first necessary to create a mental template of the steps to follow. The "Attention, Interest, Commitment, Action" ("AICA") process is an ideal formula for influencing upward in a project environment because it is systematic, memorable, and concise, with high appeal for busy decision makers. This method of persuasion is a contemporary adaptation of the popular advertising and sales process of attention, interest, desire, action (AIDA) advocated by psychologist E.K. Strong, Jr. and incorporated in the advertising body of knowledge by E. St. Elmo Lewis, the first president of the Association of National Advertisers[*]. The fundamental principle of AICA, which makes it so practical and compelling for project managers and business analysts, is that it presents a structured thinking process to formulate one's words quickly and easily. As a first step, getting the stakeholder's attention is necessary to generate interest. Once the stakeholder is interested, it is possible to motivate him or her to make a commitment. Once commitment is achieved, the consequence is that the influencer can persuade the stakeholder to agree to be accountable and to take action.

Each of the four steps in the AICA process represents a mental framework to follow:

1. *Attention:* What should they be aware of to attract their attention? The attention step addresses the key problem, risk, gain, opportunity, benefit, challenge, or vision.
2. *Interest:* What's In It For Me, or W.I.I.F.M.—The interest is a key appeal, benefit, or impact from the viewpoint of the person one is

---

[*] Strong, E.K. (1925). Theories of Selling, *Journal of Applied Psychology,* 9: 75–86.

attempting to influence. Some examples of interest-based appeals are customer satisfaction, teamwork, productivity, cost efficiency, innovation, competitive market position, stress relief, reputation, and quality.

3. *Commitment:* What information is needed to make a commitment to listen to the details and explore the problem or opportunity further? These details include the business context; the risks or gains; the methods, processes, and approaches; the options and alternatives; and the recommendation.

4. *Action:* What do you want the person you are persuading to be accountable for doing, and what are the suggested action steps? The goal for this final step is the stakeholder's agreement and accountability for moving forward with action. Summarizing next steps, roles, responsibilities, and deadlines are important details to ensure that the action takes place.

When applying AICA to "selling" the team development plan, the project manager or business analyst can organize the central message in advance very efficiently. During the actual conversation, details can be added or deleted to maintain the spontaneity of the dialogue while enabling the influencer to stay focused for maximum persuasive impact. For example, suppose Juliet, an IT call center trainer, intends to convince Steve, a project sponsor, to agree to a 10-percent increase in the team training budget for the next fiscal year. Below is an example of a core AICA message that Juliet can prepare quickly in advance of the conversation:

Attention: "I know our goal to increase our business revenue by 25 percent is important."

Interest: "By significantly increasing customer satisfaction levels, we can achieve that goal faster."

Commitment: "I require your commitment to consider implementing additional team training for our IT call center personnel, primarily in problem resolution. By improving the key source of customer complaints over the past year, we can increase customer satisfaction levels significantly."

Action: "I need your approval of a 10-percent increase in the team training budget by the end of this week and your signature on the purchase order so that we can move forward to achieve our business revenue goal."

The above AICA example illustrates the core message that Juliet can prepare for her conversation with Steve. Obviously, Steve would contribute his comments after each of the four segments and she could modify her response slightly to tailor it to the actual discussion. Although there are many alternative ways of relaying the same message, using the AICA approach maximizes the persuasive impact on senior decision makers with its focus on the overall business consequences of the recommendation. To support the impact of AICA, project managers and business analysts must have the mindset and the basic skills to influence upward.

TIPS FOR INFLUENCING UPWARD

The following five essential tips are designed to help even the most influence-challenged project managers and business analysts increase their chances of success when using AICA to influence sponsors and senior managers to approve, endorse, and support the team development plan:

1. *You have one minute:* It takes just the first minute or two in a conversation with a boss, sponsor, or other individual more senior to you to gain or lose that stakeholder's attention and interest. So use your time wisely by appealing to a key purpose or benefit first. The following are some examples of appeals generally of interest to a senior management audience in a project environment:
   - Increased productivity
   - Reduced absenteeism or turnover
   - More efficient use of resources
   - Enhanced customer satisfaction
   - More innovative decision making
   - More effective succession planning
   - Better knowledge transfer of project management and business analysis processes
   - Strategic alignment with organizational changes
2. *Train them to say "Yes":* Begin with questions that are easy for them to answer with "Yes," such as: "Do you agree that we must meet our targets?" or, "I am assuming that we need to maximize our team resources with better collaboration and decision making, right?"

When they say "Yes" to questions about the big picture, you are actually training them to say "Yes" later when you ask them to commit to more specific actions. It is necessary to gain their attention and interest first if you want their commitment and action later to support and endorse the entire team development plan.

3. *Plan your message to start at the end first:* Make it easy to understand what you want from them by the end of the discussion. Start at the end first. Begin by stating the results expected from implementing the team development plan. Then expand on related gains, losses, options, and changes. It is up to you to let your stakeholders know exactly where you want the conversation to end. Once you have focused attention on the key message, you are in the driver's seat to control the persuasion process to lead your target audience from awareness, interest, and commitment, to action.

4. *Train for the marathon:* If you were planning to run a marathon, you would probably not expect to reach the finish line without sufficient training and would begin training by running in shorter races prior to the big event. It is the same with "managing up." You also need to train ahead of time to build stamina and experience. Prepare for the marathon experience of "managing up" by creating a "managing-up" training program consisting of short spurts of persuasive discussions with sponsors and senior managers to build your experience and self-confidence. Choose topics for these conversations that are not high risk, such as asking for commitment to change a small part of a project, or recommending a project change that has a positive impact on productivity. Your goal is to build your expertise to achieve success "managing up" to sell the team development plan successfully.

5. *Practice, practice, practice!:* Do not restrict your training to actual discussions with sponsors and senior managers. Find ways to practice influencing others in your personal life as well so that you can employ the AICA process with fluency and spontaneity. Create a list of people you can practice with, including colleagues, friends, and other professionals outside of work. Try imagining they are senior to you and ask them for something. If you are a member of a professional association, club, or group, seek opportunities to practice influencing others with more authority or seniority than you and then ask for their feedback.

TIPS FOR INFLUENCING TEAM MEMBERS

Whether you manage a team of direct reports or have responsibility for members without formal authority, attaining their buy-in and commitment to the team development plan is vital. After all, this document was created primarily with the team's needs in mind. There are many positive reasons for revealing the team development plan to members. One is to generate awareness of its existence and explain its purpose in bringing about needed change to help the team achieve the team vision, mission, goals, and deliverables. Another motivation is to generate interest in providing constructive feedback for ground rules and other meeting management ideas that will be discussed later. Alternatively, relevant sections of the team development plan can provide the context to make it easier to gain the team members' commitment to participate in coaching. If the goal is to ask individuals on the team to take more accountability for leading others to achieve its performance goals, then involving them in the process of writing and revising the team development plan can be highly effective.

Regardless of one's reasons for getting buy-in and commitment for the team development plan, eight influencing guidelines should be followed for maximum impact on team members in a busy project environment:

1. People will commit to what they are connected to emotionally, so make sure team members understand how they will be affected personally as well as professionally by the team development plan.
2. Explain team goals, performance criteria, and processes cited in the plan in a unique way that team members will value and remember.
3. Give team members a sense of ownership by offering opportunities to contribute their own ideas and opinions to the team development plan so they see it as something they helped create.
4. Do not expect immediate buy-in and commitment. Give the team time to synthesize, accept, and apply each new process and change gradually.
5. Acknowledge mini-accomplishments by setting celebration milestones as each component of the team development plan is completed.
6. See it through their eyes. Empathize and ask for continuous feedback throughout all phases of organizing, implementing, evaluating, and revising the team development plan.
7. Have a realistic end goal in mind based on AICA for each influencing discussion.

8. Use the power of peer influence by encouraging team members to share their team development plan successes with their peers.

All these tips are practical ways to engage team members so they can see the value of investing their own time, energy, and resources for more effective team processes and increased performance results.

INFLUENCING TEAM MEMBERS: COMMUNICATION GUIDELINES

Table 4.1 provides communication guidelines for influencing team members.

Providing Continuous Reinforcement

There are situations when updating instead of influencing team members is warranted. The team development plan should be reviewed regularly with the team to reinforce its importance and keep it top of mind. It is important to identify opportunities to communicate relevant information related to the team development plan at project meetings and other gatherings, in emails and on intra-organizational websites. Here are some ideas for how to keep the team development plan top of mind for members in a way that has staying power.

- *Make it visual:* Display the team vision, mission, and goals on banners, flip charts, or wall hangings in meeting rooms and gathering areas visited frequently by team members to reinforce their importance and remind the team of its purpose. Publicize these on internal websites, meeting agendas and minutes, emails, reports, and other team communications.
- *Strengthen it politically:* Invite the sponsor and appropriate senior management to speak regularly at in-person and virtual meetings to emphasize the importance of topics related to the team development plan. These topics include the team vision, performance metrics, or organizational changes that impact team goals and deliverables.
- *Give it a good kick-off:* Include relevant aspects of the team development plan, such as the vision, mission, and goals, on the project kick-off meeting agenda and relevant follow-up communications.

TABLE 4.1

Influencing Team Members: Communication Guidelines

Style	Words	Time Use	Focus	DON'Ts	DO's
Results	"I" need/require: • Confident body language • Options • Risks • Money • Plan • Action	Talk to them first about: • Results • Impact	Focus on their preference for the "big picture"	Don't waste their time on problems; offer solutions instead	Challenge them: • Don't take it personally when they challenge you • Emphasize results/changes
Ideas	"I" feel/want: • "We" • Dreams • Goals • Stimulate them, make it fun	Talk to them first about: • Goals • Their fun	Focus on their preference for creativity	Don't waste their time with forms and routines	Be honest, but take time to brainstorm ideas with them
Logic	Make points in sequence: first, second, third, etc.	Talk to them first about: • Facts • Details	Focus on their preference for logic	Don't give them vague information	Try to refocus the discussion on problem solutions, instead of feelings
Routine	Focus on the task: • Ask questions • What "help" is needed • Reprioritize • Set checkpoints	Talk to them first about: • Priorities • Clear steps • Instructions	Focus on their preference for: • Job descriptions • Efficiency • Task completion	Don't waste their time by not telling them what steps to follow	Try to build trust: • Create an agenda and stay focused on issues

- *Facilitate the process:* Ensure that team interactions are facilitated consistently by balancing task and relationship activities at all meetings and discussions. Set and enforce ground rules. When necessary, acquire the services of a facilitator external to the team or the organization to establish and demonstrate appropriate norms for discussing, debating, disagreeing, and deciding.
- *Deliver it continuously:* Update the team regularly, preferably quarterly, about important messages and changes in the team development plan. Include relevant performance metrics and processes for tasks and interpersonal communications by setting expectations with each individual about what is needed to help move the team forward to the next stage of development.
- *Debrief on it:* Include debriefing discussions about team development processes, challenges, successes, and improvement ideas consistently at team meetings and individual coaching sessions.
- *Benchmark it:* Collect information about team development planning ideas and successes implemented by other organizations in similar and different fields. Share that information with the team at meetings, in emails, or by providing links to other websites.
- *Celebrate it:* Celebrate small successes with the team when team development plan milestones are achieved. This will help to reinforce the importance of team development and motivate members to continue making an effort to improve.

Reinforcing the team development plan by providing information frequently to the team and in different ways can be very effective. These activities by themselves, however, are not sufficient. To really believe in and support the team development plan through their own actions, team members need a strong leader capable of demonstrating the plan principles and practices to serve as a positive example of what they are expected to demonstrate themselves.

MODELING THE PLAN

Modeling the team development plan is a powerful form of influence because team members observe what the leader says in actions as well as with words. Modeling is not easy for project managers and business analysts, especially in project environments where the team development plan is not generally known, used, or accepted. Add to that the fact that many project leaders lack official authority over the teams they are assigned to lead; consequently, the level of difficulty in modeling the plan and its processes can be even greater. Below are some best practices for how to model the concepts and principles of the team development plan. These methods are especially applicable to individuals lacking formal authority over the teams they are responsible for leading to achieve performance goals.

- *Communicate and enforce ground rules at every team meeting:* Identify ground rules by "task" or "relationship" norms for behavior to reinforce the importance of both categories for team processes.
- *Introduce and document team processes for discussing, disagreeing, debating, and deciding*: Make these as tangible as the deadlines, requirements, and deliverables that are documented for the project.
- *Get coached:* You cannot develop the team unless you first develop your team development skills. Focus on these topics: identifying team stages and what to observe; facilitation skills at team meetings; coaching skills; conflict management skills.
- *Get observed:* Invite a certified coach or facilitator to observe you in action with your team. Ask the coach to identify strengths and areas for development to help you effectively lead team processes throughout the team's life cycle.
- *Give and solicit feedback on the team's development progress:* Give your comments on team processes that are effective and ineffective, and engage the team in evaluating itself. Consider these options: anonymous feedback on meeting effectiveness and process changes for communicating interpersonally; facilitated discussions with the team; individual interviews with team members; online surveys.
- *Adapt your communications style:* Demonstrate increased flexibility and adaptability when communicating to different styles so that you do not favor the ones most similar to yours. Teams cannot grow without diversity, and your tolerance of style differences will set the standard for others to emulate.

SUMMARY: KEY IDEAS

Concept of "Selling" the Team Development Plan

"Selling" the team development plan upward to sponsors and senior management, and downward to the team, is a necessary skill for success. The "AICA" process represents a simple, sequential framework for communicating to the project stakeholders to be persuaded, and is based on four sequential steps: Attention, Interest, Commitment, and Action. Practice AICA with colleagues, friends, and professionals outside of work to gain more competency and confidence for communicating it upward to project sponsors and senior executives.

Influencing Successfully

Influencing is a mindset as well as a skill. Remember that it only takes one or two minutes to engage someone by appealing to one of his or her interests, including: productivity, efficiency, customer satisfaction, innovation, succession planning, knowledge transfer, or strategic alignment with organizational changes. You can train them to say "yes" to sequential questions that confirm their interests before you ask for their commitment and action to support the team development plan. Beginning with the end result or key outcome first can engage others with impact. Practice for the "managing-up" marathon by attempting to persuade others in similar situations to build confidence and fluency.

Modeling the Team Development Plan

Demonstrate the importance of team development by modeling positive team behaviors and enforcing team processes that the team can observe and emulate. Give and solicit feedback on how the team's development is progressing. Demonstrate through your actions the vision, principles, and norms in the team development plan for members to observe, admire, and emulate.

5

Influencing Multigenerational Team Members

Trevor (Technical Support Specialist, age 27): *"I don't understand why you want me to wait until I have been working at this company longer and have more experience before I propose my technology solution to the CEO. I know I have been here only a short time, but I was hired for my ideas, and I want to contribute immediately by insisting on a better way to reach our goals."*

Sylvano (IT Manager, age 50): *"I have expressed to you my concerns that you need to be more of a team player. I don't think you will make a very positive impression on our senior management team if you vocalize your disagreement in the first few months of employment here without first having spent time learning the company's technology processes and understanding the reasons behind them. Your image with senior management could be affected negatively. You are risking that they could perceive you as arrogant and disrespectful, and this reputation could affect your future with this company."*

Trevor: *"I do consider myself a team player because I want to contribute my expertise so we can achieve a team goal that will help make the company more profitable."*

Sylvano: *"The CEO and senior management team have been working for this company for over thirty years. Their knowledge and experience about our processes and customers are second to none. I still think you should wait until you have learned more about our operations before you challenge their authority, especially in a public meeting setting."*

Trevor: *"I don't see that I would be challenging anyone's authority. I happen to have more technological expertise, so I just want to be sure they listen to a good idea that is worth considering, regardless of my age or experience."*

TEAMWORK: A MULTIGENERATIONAL CONCEPT

The above dialogue is based on a real-life discussion I witnessed between Trevor, a "Generation-Y" employee, and his boss Sylvano, a "Baby Boomer." Although their opposing viewpoints were influenced to some extent by their personalities, the fact that they were born in different eras also contributed to their different attitudes toward teamwork, conflict, and work priorities. Trevor's self-confidence in his knowledge of technology and his expectation that the CEO and senior management treat him as an equal are two positive traits of Generation Y. In contrast, Sylvano emphasizes the importance of work experience, knowing and respecting the history of established corporate processes, and following proper business protocol for communicating to senior management, all indicators of Baby Boomer values. Understanding these generational differences could have helped Trevor and Sylvano avoid a misunderstanding and collaborate better on a win–win approach.

The reality of multiple generations in a busy project environment is that they each have different values, beliefs, and expectations that can affect team dynamics, decision making, and productivity positively or negatively, depending on the awareness, tolerance, and adaptability of team leaders, members, and stakeholders. This chapter describes four groupings of current generations in the workforce as follows:

1. "Matures," also known as the "GI Generation" or "Traditionalists" (born 1909 to 1945)
2. "Baby Boomers" (born 1946 to 1964)
3. "Generation Xers," also known as "Baby Busters" (born 1965 to 1979)
4. "New Millennials," also known as "Generation Y's" and "Echo Boomers" (born 1980 to 2000)

These four groups have different values, motivators, work approaches, and views of "productivity" and "teamwork" that they contribute to project teams. Project managers and business analysts responsible for developing teams should become familiar with the characteristics of each generation to prevent their own biases from influencing their team interactions and decisions. Knowing more about each generation can be especially helpful for project professionals on developing teams to manage multigenerational disagreements and conflicts with more understanding, diplomacy, and flexibility.

It should be noted that the generation after the Millennials, currently known as Generation Z, Generation I, or Generation Next, is not included in this chapter because it has not yet matured enough to be adequately researched regarding workplace attitudes and behaviors. Generation Z was raised in an age of instant information and Web-based technology. Their comfort and proficiency with iPods, text messaging, smart phones, YouTube, and social communities to access through Facebook, Orkut, Twitter, Thriller, and other online streaming sites has earned them a reputation so far among researchers for being more independent, faster paced, more confident with technology, and more ambitious than their predecessors, the New Millennials. Additional time and research will reveal how they contribute to and challenge project teams[*].

MULTIGENERATIONAL CHARACTERISTICS

This section highlights the cultural interests, work values, and work strengths for each of four generations: Matures, Baby Boomers, Generation X, and New Millennials. Individual members of a generational grouping may or may not, consciously or unknowingly, believe or demonstrate these trends, so it is important to use the information for a general understanding and not for stereotyping[†].

Matures

Born between 1909 and 1945, the Matures, also known as the "GI Generation" and "Traditionalists," are disciplined, self-sacrificing, and reliable. Their generational motto can be described as "Make sacrifices, do what you are

---

[*] For more information about Generation Z, consult *Consumers of Tomorrow: Insights and Observations about Generation Z* (Nov. 2011), Grail Research, LLC, <http://grailresearch.com/pdf/conten>, accessed February 4, 2012.

[†] There are research variations in birth date data for each generation. For generally accepted dates, consult Marston, Cam. *Motivating the "What's In It For Me?" Workforce. Manage Across the Generational Divide and Increase Profits.* Hoboken, NJ: John Wiley & Sons, Inc., 2007, p. 3.

told, and exercise patience in the face of adversity." This group of individuals is resilient, patient, and resourceful. Accustomed to earning money before spending it, the Matures are diligent and hard-working employees who still have a contribution to make to project teams if they choose to work in their post-retirement years. Their career focus can be described best in these words: "Follow the rules, learn to fit in, do your part, stay in line, and you'll do fine." Regardless of whether they choose to be consultants, contract specialists, part-time subject matter experts, or small business owners, Matures have considerable talent to contribute to project teams based on their cultural experiences, work values, and work strengths outlined below.

Cultural Experiences

- Taught "waste not, want not" by their parents.
- Grew up using radio and newspapers as key sources of information. The first TV was exhibited at the World's Fair in New York City in 1945.
- First computer built at Harvard University in 1945.
- Experienced hard times during the World War I, the Great Depression, and World War II.
- "Amos and Andy" was one of the most famous radio serials.
- More than one million men from Germany, Canada, the United States, and Britain sacrificed their lives at the Battle of the Bulge on December 16, 1944, in the Ardennes Forest on the German/Belgian border.
- The Japanese bombed Pearl Harbor on December 7, 1941, and on August 6, 1945, and August 9, 1945, Americans dropped atomic bombs on the Japanese towns of Nagasaki and Hiroshima, respectively.
- The polio vaccine was developed by Jonas Salk, MD, and first administered publicly in 1954. Prior to this development, more than 20,000 cases occurred annually in North America; of those, about 1,000 people died annually from asphyxiation due to paralysis affecting their lungs.
- Heroes are Franklin D. Roosevelt and his wife Eleanor, Dwight D. "Ike" Eisenhower, Sir Winston Churchill, Douglas MacArthur and Jimmy Doolittle, Helen Keller, Clark Gable, Charles Lindbergh, Groucho Marx, and Charlie Chaplin.
- Work was an opportunity to achieve economic stability, put a roof over one's head, food on the table, and fulfill the obligation to be "responsible and community-minded adults."
- When dealing with conflict and adversity, their motto was "Grin and bear it," and the sacrifices will pay off.

Work Values

- Shame in accepting financial relief and a preference for nothing on credit.
- Dedication and sacrifice for the family.
- Conformity to social rules, government regulations, and organizational policies.
- Respect for authority.
- Delayed gratification.
- Seeking stability and security through work.
- Follow separate dress codes for work and home.

Work Strengths

- Acknowledges authority figures.
- Respects rules and regulations.
- Patience; taught to wait their turn.
- Good manners and courteous to others.
- Comfortable communicating on the phone and developing relationships with people in person.
- Accustomed to working structured hours.
- Company loyalty.
- Maturity and reliability.
- Schooled in literacy basics, especially semi-formal letter writing.
- Extensive life experience and emotional intelligence.
- Punctuality.

Baby Boomers

"We are the generation of anti-establishmentarianism" is an apt motto for the Baby Boomers, born between the years of 1946 to 1964. Witness to tremendous social, technological, and political upheaval, they played an active role in the "counterculture" of North America. Their heroes are rock stars, presidents, astronauts, and stars in the brand-new medium of television. Strong in their loyalty and work ethics, Baby Boomers are known for their initiative, self-reliance, and personalized approach to business. This generation has a primary career purpose that can be summarized as follows: "To find the most direct path to the top by working long and hard to achieve my dreams." Baby Boomers offer project teams a well-rounded

work and life experience, loyalty, and a sense of community. Their cultural experiences, work values, and work strengths are highlighted below.

Cultural Experiences

- McDonald's hamburger franchise became popular, and in 1964, a hamburger cost U.S. $0.15 at this chain.
- Television became a popular medium and most families were willing to save money to eventually purchase one.
- Popular shows were "Lassie," "Howdy Doody," "The Ed Sullivan Show," and "Gilligan's Island."
- Changes in legal and social integration, including anti-segregation laws prohibiting black Americans from being denied equal access to education, transportation, housing, entertainment, and club memberships.
- On July 20, 1969, U.S. Astronaut Neil Armstrong walked on the moon.
- The Woodstock Music Festival occurred from August 15 to 17, 1969, and was a popular generational event with approximately 500,000 participants.
- President John F. Kennedy was assassinated in Dallas, Texas, on November 22, 1963.
- Robert Kennedy and Martin Luther King, Jr. were assassinated in 1968.
- Created a "counterculture" during a time of technological and political revolution, including the Vietnam War. Their cultural interests were feminism, minority quotas, more relaxed dress codes, self-expression through music and drugs, and a high motivation for change through "sacrifice" and hard work.
- Interested in idealistic "heroes" that campaigned for social change, including John F. Kennedy and his brother Robert, Pierre Trudeau, and Dr. Martin Luther King, Jr.

Work Values

- Self-fulfillment.
- Personal gratification.
- Involvement in decision making.
- "Work Ethics" – long hours reap rewards.
- Community-oriented collaboration.

Work Strengths

- Analytical thinking and critical reasoning.
- Proactive approach to professional and personal development for self-fulfillment.
- Initiative to manage their careers and redefine themselves.
- Preference for spending time to converse with others by phone or in person.
- Fluency in oral and written, formal and semi-formal communications.
- Aware of the importance of nonverbal communication and willing to invest time in developing a personalized approach to business.
- Strong "work ethic" based on a "work to live" philosophy.

Generation Xers

The group called "Generation Xers," also known as "Baby Busters," was born between 1965 and 1979. A motto that illustrates their self-sufficiency is "I don't need someone looking over my shoulder; I know what I need to do to achieve what I want." They are known as the "latch-key kids" who watched their parents lose jobs and financial security as a result of the economic downtown of the early 1980s. Generation Xers are generally practical, realistic, and independent in spirit. This generation is not afraid to challenge authority and promote changes in working conditions and processes that support their own needs for work–life balance. Generation Xers evaluate their success in financial as well as personal gains, such as time with family and friends.

Not content to wait for years until they have saved enough money for marriage, a home, and children, this self-confident group wants it all faster and is prepared to work efficiently to get what they want. Their career aspirations can be summarized in these words: "Money is good, but to have control of my time for the people I choose to spend it with is what I envision for my future." Generation Xers can contribute many positive characteristics to project teams, including accountability, versatility, and work efficiency. Their cultural experiences, work values, and work strengths are identified below.

Cultural Experiences

- They watched their parents lose jobs or face job insecurity, so they are willing to "trade off" to establish a secure home life and more time with their children.

- As children of divorce and "latch-key kids," they were raised to be independent, self-reliant, and adaptable.
- Many entered the workplace in the early 1980s when the economy was in a downturn, so they had to be resourceful about seeking "lateral" career moves in a work setting with minimal company loyalty toward employees.
- They grew up with the introduction of PCs (personal computers).
- A popular toy line was Cabbage Patch Kids®, the most successful new doll introduction in the history of the toy industry and featured on the cover of *Newsweek* in December 1983*.
- The Berlin Wall separating West Germany and East Germany, a symbol of the Cold War built in 1961, was torn down on November 9, 1989.
- Popular television programs included "Dallas," "Magnum PI," "The Brady Bunch," and "The A Team." MTV introduced music videos and VJs to the world.
- The Chernobyl nuclear accident in the Ukraine occurred in 1986.

Work Values

- Authority should be challenged if there is a better or more efficient way to do things.
- Work is "just a job."
- Autonomy is to be enjoyed.
- Save time at work to enjoy life at home.
- Skepticism.
- Independence.
- Challenge authority figures to discover their authentic selves.

Work Strengths

- Willing to take charge of their career destiny.
- Practical.
- Efficient.
- Realists, with a special interest in integrating work with real-life experiences.
- Versatile.

---

* "Oh, You Beautiful Dolls," *Newsweek,* December 12, 1983, p. 78.

- Loyal only to the individuals they trust and respect in an organization instead of to the organization as a whole.
- More interested in life/work "balance" than more security or authority.
- Independent and not afraid to challenge authority if they can recommend a way to do things more quickly.
- Interested in heroes who are trustworthy and genuine, including Nelson Mandela, Colin Powell, Kurt Cobain, Princess Diana, David Carradine, Patrick Swayze.

New Millennials

The "New Millennials," also known as the "Echo Boomers" and "Generation Y," were born between the years of 1980 and 2000. An appropriate motto for this generation is: "We are the 'always on' generation; there is no time like the present to ask for and get what you want and deserve." The New Millennials value family, friends, technology, luxury, and work variety. Raised by parents with high expectations, they have the technological confidence and expertise, energy, and ambition to set high goals for work and life achievement. Their career aspirations are simple and can be summarized in one sentence: "I strive to avoid wasting time waiting for tomorrow when I can get it today."

The New Millennials' interest in immediate gratification enables them to work at a faster pace and adapt to change in a way that no other generation has been able to accomplish. This impatience with the status quo is largely related to the fact that this group has grown up in a fast-paced, economically unstable, and globally connected telecommunications environment where change and job insecurity are the new realities. As a less-experienced generation than Generation X and the Baby Boomers, the New Millennials bring a unique set of skills to teams. This generation excels at risk-taking, multi-tasking, technological innovation, and peer collaboration. They also respond well to coaching and knowledge-transfer opportunities that enable them to make career progress and earn more revenue faster. The cultural experiences, work values, and work strengths that generally characterize the New Millennial generation are summarized below.

Cultural Experiences

- Parents helped them plan their goals, took part in their activities, and encouraged their self-worth, so this generation has a high estimation of their capabilities.

- Recipients of the "parent as friend" and "nurture, don't lecture" child-rearing philosophy, which resulted in a strong sense of entitlement for this generation.
- Strong reliance on technology for information and entertainment that is instantaneous: online computer gaming, instant text messaging, blogging, and using high-profile Internet websites, including: YouTube © 2011, Facebook © 2011, and MySpace © 2003–2011, cell phones, BlackBerry® smart phones, iPods © 2011, and other new technological advances are necessities.
- Heroes include Mark Zuckerberg, Michael Jordan, Bill Gates, Steve Jobs, Barack and Michelle Obama, Lady Gaga, Britney Spears, Justin Timberlake, and Al Gore.
- Image conscious: enjoy showing their worth by wearing the latest labels and products to prove their status, regardless of cost.
- Demonstrate a "spend today, because there might not be a tomorrow" approach to financial management.
- Childhood toys include Power Rangers®, Captain Planet®, He-Man®, and Care Bears®.
- Grew up in an era of globalization, terrorism, the impact of the events of September 11, 2001, at the World Trade Center in New York City, global warming, corruption, rapid extinction of animal and plant species, and other related realities.
- Strong social conscience for many causes, including: AIDS, child abuse, poverty, world hunger, protecting the environment from global warming, diversity, multicultural marriages, saving animals from extinction, and medical technology to prolong lives.
- Accustomed to working in diverse groups of diverse cultures and sexual orientations from an early age.
- Prefer peer and family advice and feedback for making decisions.

Work Values

- Collaboration, especially on peer teams.
- Trust, especially with peers.
- Equal treatment by others, especially those in authority.
- Technology focused.
- Efficiency is of prime importance.
- Prefer to learn complex tasks by doing them independently, and then asking for coaching advice from those in authority when they need it.

Work Strengths

- Technology expertise and confidence.
- Comfortable communicating with their own generation.
- Willingness to take risks and to learn by trial and error.
- Multi-tasking capabilities.
- Charisma and energy.
- Fast paced when completing tasks and projects.
- Knowledge of informal communications using technology.
- Respectful of a structured, supportive work environment.
- High energy and ambition for immediate rewards.

Team Leadership Preferences

Each of the four generations envisions the ideal project team leader differently. Although beliefs about the traits of exceptional team leaders vary by individual, each generation tends to have different definitions of what makes an outstanding team leader. For Matures, a team leader who has a clear chain of command, exercises authority with confidence, and sets rules and models them by his or her own actions is someone to be respected and admired. World War II leaders such as General George MacArthur, President Dwight D. Eisenhower, and Sir Winston Churchill best illustrate those individuals who demonstrated these leadership qualities in their lifetime. In contrast, Baby Boomers are more likely to follow a democratic team leader with charisma who has ideals and seeks social change. Real-life heroes embodying these characteristics include human rights activist Martin Luther King, Jr., President John F. Kennedy, Premier Pierre Trudeau, and rock star and pacifist John Lennon of the music group called The Beatles.

For Generation Xers, preferred leaders mentor team members to be self-reliant, efficient, and pragmatic in achieving goals. These team leaders encourage work–life balance by initiating processes that boost productivity and minimize bureaucracy. Although Generation Xers are identified by many researchers as cynical and without heroes commonly admired by the entire group, they admire those who epitomize their own values, mostly within the circle of people they know professionally and personally, regardless of those individuals' ties with organizations or beliefs. Examples of ideal team leaders in the Generation X circle are current or former bosses, customers, family members, and colleagues who were successful in having an active family life and earning a good living simultaneously—without becoming workaholics or suffering burnout.

The New Millennials, in common with Baby Boomers, admire leaders who promote social causes. The distinction is that the New Millennials are more likely to respect global leaders who are multicultural, and promote the economical use of work resources. Mark Zuckerberg, the founder of Facebook©, and Al Gore, champion of global conservation, are two such examples. They are also more comfortable and fluent using technology and social networking tools such as instant messaging, Facebook©, YouTube©, Twitter©, and LinkedIn©. Some examples of heroes that the New Millennials tend to admire, and what makes the New Millennials unique in their choice of the ideal team leader, is a preference for people who are friendly and flexible coaches willing to share their work success secrets to help this group attain expertise, status, social change, and material wealth as quickly as possible.

Tips for Engaging Each Generation

Although there are many ways to engage each generation to be accountable for team development, there are a few approaches that work especially well in a project environment. The following tips are designed for project managers and business analysts interested in efficient and effective methods for motivating each generation.

Engaging Matures

1. Appeal to their interest in security, stability, and rewards for loyalty.
2. Stress the importance of duty and obligation, and communicate executive directives clearly.
3. Monitor their work pace and reassure them that they can meet deadlines when they feel time-challenged to complete tasks.
4. Provide mentoring opportunities to "pass on the wisdom" as giver and receiver.
5. Show respect in formal and personal communications.
6. Ensure frequent communications in person and by telephone, and do not overuse email.
7. Show appreciation using handwritten note cards.
8. Take advantage of coffee breaks to "chat" and develop a positive relationship.

9. Recognize the importance of a structured day with sufficient time for breaks and lunch.

10. Emphasize courtesy and be sure to say "please" and "thank you" when possible.

Engaging Baby Boomers

1. Inspire them by leading by example.
2. Offer and promote opportunities for professional recognition and personal growth.
3. Recognize and reward their "work ethic" and long work hours.
4. Ask for their advice based on their "years of experience."
5. Avoid relying too much on electronic communications; find time for personal, one-on-one conversations on the phone and in person.
6. Enable them to participate actively in open dialogues and stimulating conversations.
7. Be sure to allow time to explore methods and options in a collaborative way.
8. Practice good manners and courtesy; show respect.

Engaging Generation Xers

1. Provide and promote the most current technology for everyday use and rewards for good performance.
2. Give them as much autonomy as possible to get the job done.
3. Evaluate them on the results; do not micro-manage the details of how they accomplish these outcomes.
4. Emphasize ways to be efficient to support their "work to live" values.
5. Use efficient communications, mostly email and text messaging.
6. Empower them to be all they can be by offering opportunities to demonstrate their knowledge and practical approach.
7. Appreciate their distrust of senior management policies, directives, promises, or expectations.
8. Minimize references to rules, regulations, or bureaucracy.
9. Offer ways to trade-off work time for family time.
10. Appeal to their preference for work–life balance by evaluating them on performance, not the number of hours worked.

Engaging New Millennials

1. Provide the most recent and expensive technology for work and rewards, and use it to communicate whenever possible.
2. Reward them frequently by choosing gifts for both personal and business use that are prestigious, trendy, envied by peers, and represent the latest technology.
3. Acknowledge your appreciation for their efforts, especially when they perform tedious or overly difficult tasks that are not very stimulating for them.
4. Provide structure with clear expectations, especially about roles and results.
5. Offer opportunities to perform new, challenging, and meaningful work.
6. Explain how their work contributes to the organization in terms of its impact and importance to the vision and bottom line.
7. Emphasize their "special" qualities and importance through words and actions.
8. Make communications immediate and short.
9. Appeal to their need for instant gratification.
10. Provide ways to give and receive peer feedback, networking, and collaboration.

GENERATIONAL ALLIANCES AND CONFLICTS

Multigenerational Alliances

There are similarities between the generations that encourage intergenerational alliances. Anyone involved in developing project teams, regardless of how much or how little authority they have, should know about the most likely multigenerational alliances and how they can enhance teamwork. A knowledgeable and well-prepared project manager or business analyst who recognizes this natural synergy could take advantage of these natural connections between certain generations for team planning purposes to achieve some or all of the following outcomes:

- More in-depth and comprehensive knowledge transfer
- More active sharing and implementation of best practices

- More proactive coaching and mentoring
- More effective decision making
- More customer involvement and satisfaction
- Increased creativity for process improvements
- Stronger teamwork
- Faster adaptation to change

The most popular multigenerational alliances on project teams are explained below:

- *Matures and Baby Boomers:* What the Matures and Baby Boomers have in common is the belief that loyalty and hard work will earn them promotions, financial advancement, job security, and recognition. They also believe in the importance of taking the time to communicate in person to build trust and learning project rules and requirements before initiating recommendations for change. On project teams, Matures and Baby Boomers can be very effective mentors and coaches to share best practices about rules, regulations, guidelines, processes, and organizational politics based on their years of experience on the job.
- *Baby Boomers and New Millennials:* Baby Boomers are motivated by opportunities to share their work expertise and life experiences with others. New Millennials have an interest in being coached to acquire knowledge from others so they can progress in their own careers. Consequently, these generations partner well with each other regarding coaching-related activities. Giving advice to a generation that could be their children or grandchildren can be satisfying to Baby Boomers because they are contributing to a workforce legacy in this role. Receiving advice from someone who could be their parent or grandparent can be satisfying to New Millennials as they have an active support system to help them succeed. Consequently, Baby Boomers and New Millennials make very effective partners for succession planning, knowledge transfer, brainstorming options, and documenting historical activities on projects.
- *Generation Xers and New Millennials*: A strong connection between Generation Xers and New Millennials is based on how they both define work productivity. Multi-tasking and finding new ways to work more efficiently are important to both generations because they benefit from having more time left to dedicate to their personal lives

and interests. Their willingness to work hard in a flexible time frame can make both groups impatient at times, but they are resourceful in finding ways to better manage a large workload using technology and existing resources more efficiently. As a result, Generation Xers and the New Millennials are especially effective on projects requiring multi-tasking at a quick pace to achieve or exceed performance goals.

Multigenerational Conflicts

It is important to recognize that in addition to natural synergies between generations, there is also inherent tension and the potential for conflict between those generations that have values, expectations, and work styles contrary to each other's. The most common multigenerational conflict patterns on project teams are identified below:

- *Generation Xers and New Millennials:* Despite their common dislike for inefficiency, routine, and tedious tasks, these generations are known to clash in project environments primarily when dealing with ambiguous information, bureaucracy, managing upward, and unexpected work situations. Generation Xers prefer to handle these challenges independently with a competitive spirit that motivates them to win against all odds. New Millennials, on the other hand, tend to be more group oriented in their need for peer status and recognition to achieve goals collectively. Consequently, what a New Millennial might expect as work support, a Generation Xer could possibly misinterpret as over-indulgence. A New Millennial, however, could easily perceive a Generation Xer as a poor team player. One way to avoid unnecessary conflicts between these two generations is for the team leader to ensure that project roles and expectations are clarified and understood at the beginning of the project.
- *Generation Xers and Baby Boomers:* The Baby Boomers entered a workplace without the economic downturn that the Generation Xer faced in the 1980s, who therefore may not have had the opportunity to remain in the same company or position for many years. As a result, the Baby Boomers created a legacy of many years in the workforce that has enabled them to be effective mentors when given the chance. Yet legacy is less important to Generation Xers than expediency, and sometimes the two generations clash over this

difference. Baby Boomers value leaving a legacy of their knowledge to preserve information for the team's longevity. Generation Xers, on the other hand, can have difficulty seeing the value of talking about what was in the past when their preference is to focus more on streamlining processes for the present and future to get the work done faster so they can work fewer hours. To minimize misunderstandings and potential conflicts between Baby Boomers and Generation Xers, the team developer should provide opportunities to discuss how to better support past processes still relevant, and brainstorm ideas for new processes that are more efficient.

BUILDING MULTIGENERATIONAL COLLABORATION

A current trend in team development is a multigenerational approach to team collaboration and decision making for more innovative solutions. Each generation has a unique set of skills and insights that can help the team become more creative and produce better results. The following tips can help a team leader meld a multigenerational team into a more cohesive unit:

1. Incorporate the "Four M's" at all team interactions:
   a. Make it efficient to save time. (Generation Xers)
   b. Make it worthwhile to give input and share best practices. (Baby Boomers)
   c. Make it motivating to feel appreciated. (Generation Ys)
   d. Make sure everyone knows and follows the "ground rules" for courteous and appropriate behaviors. (Matures)
2. Implement an awareness program to acknowledge the unique contribution of each team member.
3. Establish a "buddy" system to pair different generations to share special skills and strengths.
4. Coach members individually on ways to "influence" others based on different interests, but the same goals.
5. "Rotate" team members' roles at meetings and other team activities to showcase individual talents and approaches among different generations.

6. Model competency in intergenerational communications by demonstrating an understanding of and appreciation for each generation's uniqueness.
7. Provide reading materials and resources on generational diversity, especially in one-on-one coaching and mentoring sessions.
8. Include requirements for multigenerational tolerance and adaptability on performance evaluations to ensure the issues are taken seriously and demonstrated on an ongoing basis.

SUMMARY: KEY IDEAS

The Generations

There are four generations currently on project teams that have their own values, priorities, habits, and expectations. These groupings include

1. Matures, also known as the "GI Generation," the "Silent Generation," and Traditionalists (born 1909 to 1945)
2. Baby Boomers (born 1946 to 1964)
3. Generation Xers, also known as "Baby Busters" (born 1965 to 1979)
4. New Millennials, also known as "Echo Boomers" and "Generation Y" (born 1980 to 2000)

Team Leadership Preferences

Each generation has tendencies to favor certain team leaders who use the following approaches:

Matures:	A clear chain of command
Baby Boomers:	A democratic style
Generation Xers:	An influential mentor
New Millennials:	A friendly and flexible coach

Building Multigenerational Collaboration

Key ideas for fostering team collaboration to create synergy within a multigenerational team include

- Incorporate the "Four M's": Make it efficient (Generation X); make it meaningful by taking time to share their stories and best practices (Baby Boomers); make it gratifying for self-promotion (New Millennials); and make sure everyone knows and follows the rules (Matures).
- Establish a "buddy" system to pair different generations to share skills and perspectives.
- Rotate team members' roles at meetings and other team activities to showcase different talents among the different generations.

Multigenerational Leadership Essentials

Table 5.1 highlights essential leadership approaches to implement and to avoid, especially when coaching and mentoring individual team members.

TABLE 5.1

Multigenerational Leadership Essentials

		Matures **1909–1945**		**Baby Boomers** **1946–1964**
Do's	1.	Focus on the project or task that needs to be done.	1.	Spend time getting to know them.
	2.	Emphasize the rules and restrictions.	2.	Ask them for their insights as workforce veterans with considerable experience.
	3.	Stress the practical importance for the organization.	3.	Keep them updated on all phases and changes, using a variety of media—in person, telephone, and email.
	4.	Acknowledge and reward performance and accountability in a personalized way.	4.	Appeal to ways they can contribute and increase their power and influence.
Don'ts	1.	Avoid overusing email and technology for follow-up.	1.	Don't overlook the importance of dialogue and a conversational approach, especially regarding change.
	2.	Avoid speaking too directly or quickly.	2.	Avoid overusing technology for follow-up—be sure to add a human touch.
	3.	Don't forget to say "please" and "thank you" and mean it.	3.	Don't forget to say "please" and "thank you," and mean it.
	4.	Don't expect too much risk-taking or tolerance of ambiguity.	4.	Don't overlook the importance of earning their trust by valuing their input and asking for help, even if you don't think you need it.

continued

TABLE 5.1 (continued)

Multigenerational Leadership Essentials

		Generation Xers 1965–1979		New Millennials 1980–2000
Do's	1.	Provide flexibility and freedom.	1.	Provide structure: roles and evaluation criteria.
	2.	Communicate the results expected first in a direct way.	2.	Communicate how the project or task is important to the organization, as they get discouraged easily.
	3.	Discuss how to work smarter for fewer hours invested but greater output.	3.	Incorporate peer mentoring and feedback when possible.
	4.	Appeal to self-development of "portable skills" for future opportunities.	4.	Focus on their questions and ask for their ideas first to treat them as "equals" but understand that they might be more overwhelmed than they might admit.
Don'ts	1.	Avoid pressuring them about the number of hours needed—this is a turn-off.	1.	Don't expect them to discuss things in sequential order—they like to do multiple things at once.
	2.	Don't expect them to trust senior management or company politics.	2.	Avoid lecturing or philosophizing.
	3.	Don't spend too much time talking about the company vision long-term.	3.	Don't expect them to be knowledgeable about semi-formal and formal oral and written communications; they need training and encouragement but, in exchange, can teach others lots about informal communications using technology for text messaging, etc.
	4.	Avoid micro-management: give them sufficient resources and support to get it done on their own and then debrief on ways to be more efficient.	4.	Avoid micro-management: give them a chance to learn by doing on their own and then debriefing on lessons learned.

6

Facilitating Team Development at Meetings

Erica (Engineer and Team Leader, Project X): *"My boss has just assigned me to facilitate a series of meetings with the Project X team at the conference in Atlanta next month. I am hesitant to take on this responsibility because I don't have the formal authority to do it effectively. After expressing these concerns to my boss, she recommended that I talk with you for advice and support."*

Jeremy (PMP, Director, Project Management Office): *"Why do you think you need formal authority to facilitate team meetings?"*

Erica: *"I don't think the attendees will listen to me otherwise. Most of them are senior to me, and they are used to telling their direct reports what to do. The others are colleagues who have no reason to take orders from one of their co-workers when they have their own managers to do that and set priorities for them."*

Jeremy: *"I can appreciate those concerns, especially if you were going to be leading the meetings. But you are going to be facilitating the meetings, which is very different. You do not need formal authority to be an effective facilitator. Your role is to listen to what the attendees say, not the other way around."*

Erica: *"I am a good listener, and my boss thinks I am very process oriented. But I am just a solitary project team leader on the hierarchical food chain."*

Jeremy: *"Actually, the role of facilitator is ideal for someone like you who is a good listener. Your role is to uncover other people's ideas and enforce the facilitation process; both will give you power without your needing a title."*

Erica: *"There is also the question of time. I am concerned about how long it will take me to prepare when I have so many other tasks to complete."*

Jeremy: *"Facilitating is actually more efficient to plan than you think. Once you know your objectives and expected outcomes, you can plan the process for the discussion or activity quite efficiently. I don't think it will take you as long as you expect."*

Erica: *"Well, I still need to think about it."*

FACILITATION POWER

In the above dialogue, Jeremy challenges Erica to change her paradigm about power. He encourages her to think beyond her title and level of authority to a higher level of influence. Erica's process-oriented approach and good listening skills can work in her favor if she uses these skills to her advantage. Jeremy recognizes that Erica has the capacity to use this type of facilitative power to build better team discussion and improve decision making. Although she views it as a disadvantage, Erica's process-oriented approach and lack of seniority could actually work to her advantage by enabling her to remain neutral and focused throughout the meeting. These all add up to Erica's potential power as a facilitator. The following quote from a facilitation expert explains this kind of power very clearly by saying:

> "When leaders shift their paradigm from controlling and directing to facilitating and empowering, they often feel as though they have given up all of their familiar 'power tools.' In reality, there is a substantial amount of power and control built into the role of facilitator. The difference is that this power is exerted indirectly, through the application of process, rather than through direct control."[*]

The true power of effective facilitators is revealed when they create an open and trusting environment where all team members feel free to contribute their ideas and skills to help achieve a common goal. Whether they are in person or virtual, well-facilitated meetings are an efficient and

---

[*] Bens, Ingrid. *Facilitating with Ease!*, San Francisco, CA: Jossey-Bass, 2000, p. 27.

effective way to increase member accountability and participation in the team's development and overall progress. For this reason, facilitation functions as the glue that helps members develop to discuss, disagree, debate, and decide better at all stages of team development.

FACILITATING AS A PROCESS

The most effective project team facilitators are committed to observing, guiding, engaging, encouraging, and challenging a team to focus on mutual goals and interests for discussion and problem solving. They must be skilled at questioning, listening, affirming, adapting, and synthesizing ideas and solutions. Facilitated discussions and activities should be planned and implemented in as many team meetings and interactions as possible to pave the way for the team to progress through its life cycle.

Facilitation can include any or all of the following communications processes: questioning, paraphrasing, self-reflection, synthesizing ideas, brainstorming, debating, decision making, problem solving, discussing, disagreeing, and debriefing on lessons learned. The checklist in Table 6.1 identifies these responsibilities in more detail.

TABLE 6.1

Checklist of Facilitator Responsibilities

- Remain "neutral" in point of view: You are the catalyst, not the key focus.
- Create a "Parking Lot" for details to address later.
- Summarize key points and make them visual.
- Help the group stay focused on the outcomes.
- Establish and encourage a group process for disagreeing without arguing.
- Establish and encourage a group process for making key decisions.
- Summarize what was suggested.
- Encourage active participation from everyone.
- Create and maintain a positive team climate.
- Ensure that all three learning styles are addressed (hearing, seeing, doing).
- Get commitment and agreement on next steps.
- Ask more questions and make fewer statements.
- Break teams into sub-groups at times to enhance participation.
- Encourage, affirm, support, repeat, rephrase, ask "what if" questions.

Leading versus Facilitating Meetings

In his conversation with Erica, Jeremy distinguished between the roles of *leading* and *facilitating* meetings. Both roles are important for developing teams, and in some circumstances, meeting leaders are also the facilitators. However, because each role is quite different and requires a distinct set of skills that can at times contradict each other, it is a best practice to assign different individuals to assume each role. These differences are highlighted in Table 6.2.

TABLE 6.2

Leading versus Facilitating Skills

Leading:	
Primary focus:	Meeting content
Emphasis:	Staying on agenda, status updating, decision making, problem solving, ensuring accountability for action
Topics of interest:	Purpose, objectives, constraints, scope of authority, moving the project forward, achieving project deliverables
Skills:	Efficiency, decisiveness, clear focus on what needs to be done at the meeting, comprehensive and evaluative listening, content awareness and knowledge, awareness of the time constraints, budget, requirements, resources, and deadlines for projects
Facilitating:	
Primary focus:	Balancing task and relationship processes for maximum participation by all attendees
Emphasis:	Establishing and sustaining a positive emotional climate
Topics of interest:	Effective processes for team sharing, deciding, agreeing, disagreeing, debating, problem solving, brainstorming, and collaborating
Skills:	Empathy, critical and empathetic listening, knowledge of different learning styles, synthesizing ideas, technical training in group dynamics and processes; team development expertise; skills in conflict management, influencing, questioning, collaboration methods, time management

CREATING GROUND RULES

Ground rules are the facilitator's primary tool for enforcing task and relationship processes without being too controlling or authoritative. Ground rules are essential for gaining buy-in and commitment from team members to be accountable for the meeting outcomes and actively participate in the process. They are especially important in virtual meetings where it is difficult from a distance to keep members engaged and control disruptive and disrespectful behaviors.

The extent of team involvement in creating the ground rules depends on the life cycle of the team. For forming or storming teams, facilitators should present the ground rules and ask team members to contribute any additional suggestions. When facilitating meetings for norming teams, it is better for the team to create its own ground rules and for the facilitator to suggest additions, if any. At meetings with performing or adjourning teams, the facilitator should ask the team to create its own ground rules and then evaluate their effectiveness in following them.

Ideally, ground rules contain a balance of task and relationship activities to establish an atmosphere that encourages participation. Ground rules that focus solely on task activities are not suitable for a facilitated meeting because they do not require participants to take responsibility for how their behaviors and communications impact on others. To ensure that the team gains maximum benefit from the ground rules, project professionals should include an equal number of task and relationship guidelines based on some or all of the details below. The following are examples of questions to consider when creating ground rules that contain a balance of tasking and relating guidelines:

1. Getting Things Done (Tasking):
   - What are the group processes for time efficiencies?
   - How will the team stay focused to cover the agenda contents?
   - How will the team make decisions during the meeting?
   - What are the limits for using technology such as computers and phones when the meeting is in session?
   - How to address interruptions or digressions from the main topic?
   - What process will be used for deciding about tasks?
2. Interacting with Others (Relating):
   - How to help everyone feel safe and comfortable participating?
   - How to appeal to different learning styles?
   - How to manage dominating, disruptive, and negative behaviors?
   - What group processes will be used for discussing, disagreeing, and debating?
   - How to build rapport and trust among team members?

TABLE 6.3

Sample Ground Rules for Task and Relationship Activities

Ground Rules	T	R
• Pace = 80/20 rule	X	
• Start/end and return from breaks on time	X	
• Respect others' different styles		X
• If you prefer not to answer a question, say "I'm thinking"		X
• One person speaks at a time		X
• All questions welcome	X	X
• "Parking Lot" to list questions and follow-up required	X	X
• Cell phones, computers, and other electronics off/on vibrate	X	

Sample Ground Rules

The ground rules offered in Table 6.3 above and illustrated in the paragraph below how to balance task (T) and relationship activities (R).

Enforcing Ground Rules

Facilitators need to ensure that participants follow ground rules and, when necessary, take action to remedy any deviations. Obviously, some methods for reminding attendees to follow ground rules will be different for in-person meetings than for virtual meetings held on Skype, by teleconference, or other virtual meeting software. For in-person meetings, it is easier to see signs of inattention to the ground rules, such as a participant using a cell phone or two individuals conversing while someone else is speaking. When this happens, the facilitator can take control nonverbally by moving to the attendees' seating area, establishing eye contact, or meeting with them individually during a break to refocus their attention. In virtual meetings, however, facilitators need to take action in different ways.

Table 6.4 provides tips for enforcing ground rules successfully for in-person and virtual meetings, as appropriate.

Facilitator Competencies

In addition to enforcing ground rules, skilled facilitators engage all team members by focusing on accommodating different learning styles; maintaining a positive tone and high energy level; helping the group focus on the topic; adjusting the pace; paraphrasing what was said so the group can hear it and reflect on it; initiating, executing, monitoring, and controlling

TABLE 6.4

Enforcing Ground Rules at Meetings

Ground Rule	IP*	V*
• Email the ground rules to each attendee prior to the meeting and ask for input regarding any additional items to add.	X	X
• When primarily using PowerPoint for the meeting, ensure that the ground rules are included in a prominent location.	X	X
• State the ground rules at the beginning of the meeting and remind attendees about them after any breaks.	X	X
• Enforce ground rules immediately after they are not followed, such as reminding people to state their names each time they talk, if that is a ground rule.	X	X
• Use real-time opportunities to "chat" with individuals online during the meeting if there are issues about ground rules you need to discuss with them.		X
• Remind participants to use their mute buttons to avoid distracting noises or interruptions during the meeting.		X

Note: IP, in person; V, virtual.

group processes for discussing, debating, disagreeing, and deciding; and intervening in case of tension or conflict. These can be separated into eight key activities:

1. Managing expectations
2. Building relationships
3. Appealing to styles
4. Modeling the process
5. Questioning and listening
6. Keeping others focused
7. Fostering collaboration
8. Managing resistance and conflict

Managing Expectations

Before the Meeting:

1. Circulate surveys to identify participant perceptions, needs, and expectations.
2. Interview participants to build rapport and identify learning requirements.
3. Read background reports on business challenges and issues.

4. Send an advance email to explain the purpose of the event.
5. Request participants' comments on the agenda and other topics of interest.
6. Ask for participant feedback about some of the intended facilitation objectives, strategies, or tactics.
7. Consider participants' styles and how you can adapt.

During the Meeting:

1. Explain your role and how you will help to engage the audience.
2. Create a "safe" atmosphere by seeking feedback and getting agreement for ground rules.
3. Be sure to include a "Parking Lot" to list topics for more detailed discussion later.
4. If appropriate, assign a note taker.
5. Set time frames and evaluate progress periodically. If appropriate, assign a timekeeper.
6. Stay neutral; do not agree or disagree.
7. Ask questions, paraphrase, listen actively, and demonstrate empathy.
8. Observe learning styles and adjust accordingly when needed.
9. Ask for feedback about the pace.
10. Keep the group aware of progress.
11. Listen for what is not said and adapt accordingly.
12. Emphasize mutual interests whenever possible.
13. Use previews and summaries periodically to keep interest and help participants communicate their questions, ideas, lessons learned, and next steps.
14. Make sure you do not overuse physical barriers to your audience, such as a podium or desk. When possible, step away or walk into the audience and talk with them. If you can, place the podium to one side of the room so you can walk around it.

After the Meeting:

1. Review evaluations and look for trends in participants' perceptions of what was effective and ineffective.
2. Provide participants with post-meeting work for applying what was covered at the session and/or additional ideas and feedback.

3. Communicate to the participants what you learned from them and how you will apply their feedback the next time you facilitate.

4. Evaluate the structure and processes you used and generate an action plan for what you will do the same or differently in the future.

Appealing to Styles

Another way to engage participants is to adapt your delivery style to appeal to the three learning styles. These three learning styles are visual, auditory, and tactile. The tips below offer many different options for appealing to each learning style for increased engagement among attendees:

1. Visual learners:
   - Use visual materials such as pictures, charts, maps, graphs, etc.
   - Give a clear view of presenters so participants can see their body language and facial expressions.
   - Use color to highlight important points in the text.
   - Take notes or ask presenters to provide handouts.
   - Illustrate ideas as a picture or brainstorming visual before writing them down.
   - Write a story and illustrate it.
   - Use multimedia for variety and added interest.
   - Study in a quiet place away from verbal disturbances.
   - Read illustrated books.
   - Visualize information as a picture to help remember key ideas.
2. Auditory learners:
   - Participate in discussions/debates.
   - Make speeches and presentations.
   - Use a tape recorder during lectures instead of taking notes.
   - Read text aloud.
   - Create musical jingles to aid memorization.
   - Create mnemonics to aid memorization.
   - Discuss ideas verbally.
   - Dictate to others while they write down your thoughts.
   - Use verbal analogies and storytelling to demonstrate important concepts.
3. Tactile learners:
   - Get involved physically as well as mentally.
   - Take frequent breaks.

- Move around while learning (e.g., break into sub-groups, use props to get the message across).
- Use bright colors to highlight visuals and reading material.
- Fill the meeting space with posters and colorful visuals.
- Give them time to skim through reading material to get a rough idea regarding what it is about before addressing it in detail.
- Let them try things first, then give them instructions or input later.

The Four Ds

The "Four D's" method is an easy way to remember and apply a facilitative process at team meetings, either virtual or in person. The Four D's signify discussing, debating, deciding, and debriefing. Each of these D's involves key questions the facilitator must address, either independently or in consultation with team members, to determine the group processes for the meeting. These questions are outlined below:

Discussing:

1. What is the key problem or issue to be discussed?
2. What group process will be used for the discussion: writing down questions, pairing up with someone, flipcharts, giving everyone a turn to speak?
3. What kind of seating is required to encourage participants at all levels in the organization to interact equally with one another?
4. Who will lead the discussion?
5. How to ensure everyone's input so that no one dominates?
6. How will attendees support each other to communicate their viewpoints openly?
7. What guidelines do attendees need to listen actively to each other to improve understanding or avoid tangents?

Debating:

1. What group process will be used to encourage differing views and ideas and enable them to be heard?
2. What can be done to ensure that disagreement does not escalate into retaliation or conflict?

3. How will key points of disagreement be captured so they are accessible to all team members?
4. How will the facilitator create a "safe" environment to encourage diverse perspectives?

Deciding:

1. What method(s) will the team use to make decisions collectively?
2. How does the team ensure that it has considered all relevant options before deciding?
3. How does the facilitator enable the team to make good decisions that are aligned strategically?

Debriefing:

1. What process will work best for team members to evaluate how well they discussed, debated, and decided?
2. What evaluation guidelines will be used to assess the discussion, debating, and decision making?
3. How frequently will the debriefings take place?
4. Who will lead the discussion?
5. What methods will be used to acquire feedback from team members to assess the debriefing process and recommend improvements?

Questioning and Listening

Experienced facilitators know that asking questions and listening, rather than doing most of the talking, maximizes audience participation. Varying the types of questions asked is especially important in virtual meetings to keep audiences actively involved and make it easier for participants to maintain interest. An effective way to engage team members at meetings is to alternate between using "open" and "closed" questions without over-using each type. The differences are identified below:

Open Questions

Example: "What are some of the team challenges you are experiencing with Project W?"

1. Cannot be answered with "Yes" or "No"
2. Usually start with "Why?" or "How?"
3. Useful for obtaining lots of information
4. Useful for opening a conversation

Risks: It takes time for some people to organize their thoughts, and some individuals could have difficulty interpreting the question under pressure.

Closed Questions

Example: "Do you prefer to lead the team, or would you like someone else to do that?"

1. Can be answered with "Yes" or "No"
2. Often ask the individual to decide between two specific options
3. Useful for obtaining the specific information required
4. Useful for getting information quickly

Risks: If this type of question is over-used, the questioner could be viewed as being too inquisitive or demanding.

Clarifying Questions

Facilitators can use clarifying questions to encourage more team participation. Examples of clarifying questions are indicated below:

1. Ask for a review of progress made:
   Examples:
   > "Fred, you don't appear to be in agreement on this point. Would you please summarize your key objections?"
   > "I've heard a lot of good ideas in the past twenty minutes. Could you identify which ones are the key ideas you would like to address as part of this project?"
2. Refocus the participant's attention:
   Examples:
   > "Are we on the right track here?"
   > "Are there any other ways to accomplish this?"

3. Address differences of opinion directly:

   Examples:

   > "Gerry, I am sensing you are hesitant to make a commitment. Could you explain what is holding you back?"

   > "Ed, you indicated at our last meeting that you had no trouble committing to this; now you are hesitant. Could you please help me understand what has changed or what you are concerned about?"

4. Ask for consensus:

   Examples:

   > "Lee, we have covered five items this morning. Let's review them to be sure we are in agreement."

   > "Is your decision one that you believe the senior management committee in your organization will support and accept?"

5. Ask about the impact:

   Examples:

   > "How do you think this technical change will impact our customers?"

   > "How will this revision affect the meaning of the document?"

6. Ask for their perspective:

   Examples:

   > "What is your thinking on …?"

   > "Would you tell me more about …?"

7. Ask for elaboration:

   Examples:

   > "John, could you explain this again?"

   > "Please tell me more.…"

8. Paraphrase into a new question:

   Examples:

   > "Ivan, could you please restate what you just said for clarification?"

   > "If I understand this correctly, you are saying .…"

9. Ask "what-if" questions:

   Examples:

   > "Lynn, if you could choose the top three, what would your choices be?"

   > "What if we were to outsource that service?"

10. Ask "Why?" or "Why not?":

    Examples:

    > "Tell me why you think management does not care?"

    > "Why do you think this procedure is not right for this situation?"

Keeping Others Focused

Effective facilitators know how to phrase their comments so they flow in a cohesive way to help others listen and stay focused. The following methods are especially useful in virtual meetings because they keep the discussion flowing and the participants actively engaged:

Transitions

Transitions are words or phrases that indicate when a presenter has completed one thought and is moving on to another one. They usually involve both what was discussed and what will be discussed. Examples include

1. "In addition to…, also…."
2. "Only one part…, the other part…."
3. "Now that we have…, let's review…."
4. "So much for…, what about…?"
5. "We have spent time discussing…; now it is time to…."

Internal Previews

Internal previews or forecasts are the key points you will discuss with your audience. Examples include

1. "In discussing the problem of why facilitators are often so nervous, we shall first examine what nervousness is; second, how it occurs; and third, how to manage it."
2. "I will concentrate on three aspects of signposts: what they are, how they are worded, and how to use them effectively when facilitating."

Internal Summaries

Internal summaries are the reverse of internal previews. They remind your audience of what they just heard to help them listen better, retain the information, and stay focused on the discussion. Internal summaries are generally useful when finishing an important main point or set of main points. Internal summaries are often followed by a transition, as shown in the following example:

"Let's pause for a moment and review what we have discovered so far. First, we have discussed that most inexperienced facilitators underestimate the importance of audience needs; second, we have explored what an audience expects from a facilitator; and third, how these expectations frequently differ tremendously from the facilitator's expectations. *(Transition)* Now we are ready to uncover some practical techniques to establish confidence and audience rapport when facilitating outcomes effectively."

Signposts

Signposts are words or statements updating the audience about meeting milestones related to the meeting schedule or issues discussed. Facilitators typically use signposts to help the audience listen, remember, and apply what is discussed. Examples include

1. "Finally, we have reached our conclusion…."
2. "The first issue is…."
3. "The second issue is…."
4. "The final issue is…."
5. "Next, we will discuss…."
6. "The most important question to remember is …."
7. "Be sure to remember that…."
8. "Above all, these are the three key points we agreed to…."
9. "Before we take a break…."

Building Collaboration

The best way for a facilitator to build collaboration on teams is to generate opportunities for members to problem-solve by being soft on the person and hard on the problem. Emphasizing a collaborative mindset is the first step, followed by encouraging collaborative language and problem solving based on mutual interests. The guidelines below identify ways for project professionals to foster team collaboration efficiently and effectively at team meetings. The key is consistency and frequency.

1. Know your objective(s) and key issues, and stay focused.
2. Use "we" language and avoid assigning blame.
3. Set the right tone to be in the "aim frame" and not the "blame frame."

4. Disengage emotionally and focus on the underlying causes of problems instead of the external symptoms.
5. Emphasize mutual interests and benefits.
6. Support your proposed options and recommendations by facts.
7. Don't take it personally.
8. Remain confident and convincing.
9. Concede on any items of least importance to you/the organization.
10. Be sure to confirm what was agreed upon.
11. Emphasize the integration of ideas as more important than agreement.

Managing Resistance and Conflict

Experienced facilitators know that team tension and conflict at meetings is inevitable, and that these situations must be managed carefully with assertiveness and tact. In a hectic project environment, team members sometimes bring their own insecurities, frustrations, fears, political leanings, and stress reactions to meetings. The atmosphere can become tense if these individuals lack the self-control, awareness, assertiveness, or diplomacy to handle team disagreement and conflict appropriately. In addition to enforcing ground rules for appropriate task and relationship behaviors, facilitators can manage resistance and conflict in person or virtually by refocusing the team on what matters most.

Guidelines for Managing Conflict responses

- Emphasize "us against the problem" instead of "me against you."
- Communicate and enforce ground rules to handle disagreement.
- Listen for opportunities to emphasize agreement on mutual interests, such as improving performance or increasing customer satisfaction, instead of differing positions, such as different expectations about requirements, methodologies, deadlines, and priorities.
- Call a break if necessary to diffuse tension or conflict that is not constructive and address pressing issues one-on-one during the break without an audience.
- Ask the team to help identify the common need or goal that ultimately connects them, such as agreeing that there needs to be a better process, or recognizing that the methodology should be reexamined.

- Be aware of your own conflict responses and manage them by staying focused, taking mental and physical breaks, getting coaching assistance, and obtaining feedback.

SUMMARY: KEY IDEAS

Facilitating at Meetings: An Essential Team Development Skill

The ability to facilitate team processes by balancing tasks with relationships is an essential skill for project professionals to master to develop the team proactively through its life cycle. It is not necessary to have authority or seniority to facilitate team processes effectively at meetings. What it does take is the commitment to follow a process consistently using the "Four D's"—for discussing, debating, deciding, and debriefing. Communicating and enforcing ground rules are the facilitator's primary tools to establish accountability for supporting team members through active listening and participation, especially in virtual meeting situations.

When project team facilitators encounter resistance and conflict, it is important to emphasize "us against the problem" instead of "me against you." Communicating and enforcing norms for appropriate behavior, thinking and saying "and" instead of "but," remaining neutral while acknowledging concerns, and listing unaddressed issues on a "parking lot" are all best practices. Above all else, facilitators need to manage their own conflict responses by taking physical and mental breaks, demonstrating the processes they recommend, acquiring coaching assistance, and obtaining feedback for continuous improvement.

7

Team Succession Planning

Patti (Project Sponsor): *"What steps are you currently taking for team knowledge transfer?"*

Bert (Project Manager): *"We have a team knowledge-sharing website that everyone on the team is required to update weekly. It enables us to identify mandatory, discretionary, and external dependencies for the project, increase our productivity, and avoid task duplication."*

Patti: *"What information does it contain?"*

Bert: *"Key tasks completed, action steps, technical knowledge, resources including templates and references, and client data."*

Patti: *"So the key focus is on the team members' project tasks and subject matter expertise?"*

Bert: *"Yes."*

Patti: *"What about the other aspects of the team's 'brain' of knowledge?"*

Bert: *"Like what?"*

EVALUATING THE TEAM "BRAIN" OF KNOWLEDGE

The above conversation highlights one of the biggest team development opportunities that project professionals face today: team knowledge transfer for better productivity and performance. Key factors contributing to this opportunity include the pending retirement of Baby Boomers and the need to acquire their knowledge before they leave the workforce, too much information to share due to the increased speed and volume of data available from new technologies, and limited access to team members due to geographical dispersion and virtual working arrangements. Regardless of the amount of time their members work together and the specific stage of development they progress to, most teams will benefit from some type of knowledge sharing. In Bert's case, he recognizes that his team members need to share access to technical, operational, and business information that will enable them to perform better.

According to Jim Muckle, Chief Learning Officer at BrainsInAction Inc. and author of *The Ultimate Brain,* the "team brain" is vital to the longevity of teams and the organizations they support. Muckle states,

> "The effectiveness of the 'Team Brain' can be measured by looking at the level of individual and team competencies around these aspects of learning: sorting through available information to find what's useful; understanding that information so that it becomes useful knowledge; storing that understanding; recalling that understanding; applying that understanding to impact the 'bottom line' of the team or organization. Practical application is the only true test of understanding."*

What Bert includes in his list of topics for knowledge transfer emphasizes concrete, precise, explicit, and systematic details related to the project, all representative of left-brain thinking. The left-brain mindset is sequential, linear, compartmentalized, ordered, objective, and detailed, using checklists and templates. Left-brainers prefer to document information and data in writing, and they tend to have a low tolerance for ambiguity. When Patti asks Bert to tell her about any other aspects of the team's "brain" of knowledge, she is implying that he has omitted other options that are important. Bert is so left-brained in his thinking at that moment that he is not readily aware of any other options to consider.

Essentially, Bert did not factor into his plan for team knowledge transfer any approaches from the right-brain thinking style. In contrast to left-brain thinking, right-brain thinking is spontaneous, intuitive, non-sequential, holistic, subjective, and very difficult to convert to left-brain tools such as checklists and templates. Right-brainers tend to distrust written documentation in favor of verbal agreements that they are comfortable with intuitively. In addition, right brainers generally have a higher tolerance for ambiguity than left-brainers.

Ideally, the team "brain" of knowledge will be a composite of both left- and right-brain perspectives concerning people, processes, technology, problem solving, and decision making in order to balance all possible perspectives. One of the best ways to fully understand each brain style is to

---

* Jim Muckle, interview, August 3, 2011.

analyze real-life examples of teams when they were used effectively. These examples appear below:

- *People: Knowing the personal preferences and needs of management, stakeholders, customers, and vendors.*

  Example: Mary, an important customer, prefers meeting on Tuesdays or Wednesdays and only during the hours of 8:30 a.m. to 11:45 a.m. John, a business developer bidding on a team project for Mary that is worth $1 million, has accommodated this need, as well as other preferences, throughout three years of working with her on a variety of projects.

  When John leaves the company for a new position and Fred replaces him as Mary's key contact, Fred does not know about Mary's preferences. After Fred insists on meeting with Mary on a few consecutive Thursdays at 9:00 a.m. due to his busy schedule, Mary gets frustrated. She expects John to know her routine—the one that she established with John during the three years they worked together. Soon afterward, Mary informs Fred that she has decided to hire a different company. Fred's team loses a major contract with a previously loyal customer and now has new pressures to replace this business for similar revenues.

  (Mary's scheduling preference is a left-brain example; her decision to hire a new vendor who understands her requirements is also left-brain.)

- *Processes: Knowing about a best practice, procedure, or methodology for team projects that has been implemented over time by one or more individuals that is neither known nor implemented by the rest of the team.*

  Example: Carl has a verbal agreement with the purchasing manager at an important vendor that anything Carl purchases for his team qualifies for a 5% discount. Carl decides to take early retirement and move to France. A few months after he leaves the organization, the company receives a bill for $20,000 in unpaid charges for orders delivered that past year. Because no one on the team knew about Carl's verbal agreement, and the purchasing manager at the vendor's organization was fired, the bill had to be paid and the team had to cancel its annual training event due to lack of funding.

(Carl's verbal agreement with the purchasing manager is primarily right-brain, but the company's decision to bill him for outstanding expenses because the agreement was not documented in writing is left-brain.)

- *Technology: Knowing about a specific technology that no one else on the team is aware of, or knows how to use.*

    Example: Jerry has been responsible for a computer mainframe for many years and is the only person on the team who knows how to fix it when it is not functioning properly. Despite attempts during the past year to convince Jerry to document his knowledge for his colleagues to access, he has ignored those requests. Nonetheless, Jerry complains frequently about wasting valuable time repairing the system because other team members rely on him.

    (Jerry's preference to be the subject matter expert and his reluctance to share this information with others is a left-brain tendency. As a left-brainer, Jerry could also be trying to protect his job security by ensuring that he is the only person on the team who can do that job.)

- *Problem-Solving: Associative thinking to solve problems involves knowing about topics that are not directly related to the individual's job, and using that information to influence the way he or she solves problems, makes decisions, and interacts with others.*

    Example: Becky is a business analyst who has always had a special interest in gardening, especially landscape design based on European castles. Recently she collaborated with a team member to solve a mainframe and software compatibility problem between her organization's and the client's computers. Without knowing why, Becky thought about a specific design she had just created for her garden, but instead of drawing shrubs and flowers, she drew a "landscape" of patterns in various shapes, sizes, and configurations, each one representing an idea. When she completed this drawing, Becky realized that she had actually created a visual representation of how to approach the computer compatibility issue. She then reorganized the visuals in sequential order. Becky and her colleagues were amazed when the project sponsor approved the design, with slight modifications, based on Becky's drawing spawned by her personal interest in landscape gardening.

(Becky used a right-brain thinking approach of free association with landscaping, but her decision to revise the drawing into sequential order was a left-brain approach.)

- *Decision Making: Emotional agility is an important element of decision making. Knowing how to demonstrate resiliency and flexibility emotionally when dealing with resistance, conflict, and change can help ensure more effective decision making on a project team.*

    Example: Jill continues to be assigned high-profile projects in a highly political work environment because she is resilient and adaptable under pressure. She focuses more on the "big picture" of what must be done and ignores details that are not pertinent to the mission or goal. She also relies a lot on her intuition to help her make decisions about how to handle unexpected situations. The issue is that her workload is 40 percent more than her colleagues' workload because management is not confident that anyone else on her team can handle her workload. Although her colleagues are more proficient technically in some ways, they lack her level of emotional resiliency and have demonstrated difficulties coping with change. Although Jill is flattered by the confidence her superiors have in her abilities, she is applying for jobs at other organizations where she hopes to be rewarded with more challenging assignments instead of being overloaded with work that she does not find especially fulfilling anymore.

    (Jill's reliance on intuition to decide how to handle unexpected situations is an example of right-brain thinking.)

TEAM "BRAIN DRAIN"

A project developer's inattention to any of the above categories can contribute to team "brain drain." This phenomenon occurs when individual knowledge is not fully developed or transferred within the team. "Brain drain" is caused by either inadequate information-sharing processes or a preoccupation with short-term crises, resulting in failure to invest time on succession planning within the team. Jim Muckle explains it as an absence of shared learning: "When shared learning does not take place, there will likely be a 'brain drain' when one or more team members depart."[*]

"Brain drain" can be harmful to teams and their organizations. First, it can prevent the team from ever attaining its full potential to utilize the knowledge and talents of its members for the benefit of the entire unit. The team will have difficulty reaching self-sufficiency because its growth will be stunted and it will never achieve the performing stage of its life cycle. Second, the team and the organization risk losing talented and ambitious team members. Unable to fulfill their professional goals or to learn from others, they choose to work elsewhere, where they will be challenged to contribute their skills and pursue their career interests. Finally, those team members who have not benefited from knowledge transfer within the team could unknowingly contribute to its "brain drain" by isolating themselves, withholding information from others, and refusing to adapt new methods to stay current. The following best practices for knowledge transfer between members can help project managers and business analysts tap into the inherent wisdom of their teams.

Guidelines for Team Knowledge Transfer

To Do

1. Ensure that the action plan for team knowledge transfer supports the team vision, mission, and goals.
2. Include an oral knowledge transfer segment that is documented in writing at each team meeting. Include it in the meeting minutes for archival purposes.
3. Arrange for each team member to present his or her ideas of best practices for any or all of the following: people, processes, technology, associative thinking, and emotional agility.
4. Assign a "backup" person or "buddy" to each team member to share best practices.
5. Implement a team coaching and mentoring program to encourage continuous personal and professional development based on a team knowledge-sharing plan.
6. Sponsor opportunities for learning from other teams and professionals external to the organization to expand team knowledge in new areas.

---

[*] Ibid.

7. Communicate appropriate information about knowledge transfer goals, processes, and opportunities to the team and senior management, at least quarterly.

8. Continuously ask members for suggestions about how to transfer individual knowledge to the entire team and follow through on implementing some of their ideas.

9. Schedule consistent coaching and mentoring activities over an extended period of time to enable team members to absorb and apply what is learned.

10. Ensure that team members receive some cross-functional training and development outside of their technical and professional areas, especially general business skills, to help them become more articulate and influential in their communications.

11. Use a variety of record-keeping and documentation options, including job diaries, progress reports, charts, diagrams and templates, checklists, surveys, photographs, and other visuals.

12. Include knowledge transfer as a required team norm and job performance requirement.

13. Assign job shadowing and temporary assignments enabling team members to act on one another's behalf for knowledge transfer.

14. Celebrate small improvements and best practices on the team to reward knowledge transfer among members.

15. Recognize and reward members for initiating knowledge transfer opportunities.

16. Implement a team event featuring a "saying good-bye to the past" ritual dedicated to setting new goals for team knowledge exchange.

To Avoid

- Omitting people, processes, technology, associative thinking, and emotional agility as components of the team's knowledge transfer plan
- Depending too much on one or two individuals on the team to be the central repository for team knowledge
- Ignoring opportunities to discuss and explore team members' experiences and approaches to develop emotional agility to manage project setbacks, conflicts, and changes
- Relying too much on written documentation about project facts, data, and tasks to capture team knowledge
- Encouraging team members to restrict their thinking to their subject matter expertise only

- Eliminating team opportunities for associative thinking to generate options for more effective problem solving
- Assuming that team knowledge must be logically "relevant" to be valuable
- Showing preferential treatment to team members based on their seniority, credentials, or assumed technical expertise
- Underestimating how threatening knowledge sharing can be to team members, especially individuals fearing job replacement or redundancy

KNOWLEDGE TRANSFER METHODS

There are many methods for achieving knowledge transfer on project teams. The following are common options to consider:

1. Create a knowledge transfer policy statement:
   - Communicate team standards for conduct, policies, and procedures related to knowledge transfer.
   - Ensure that the policy statement follows legal requirements for confidentiality.
   - Ensure that the policy is accessible to appropriate stakeholders through a variety of media.
2. Publicize a process for expanding team knowledge:
   - Make it visual and accessible to all team members.
   - Encourage team members to challenge existing knowledge constructively.
   - Communicate the positive intentions of the organization and the team sponsor.
3. Develop an efficient system for record-keeping:
   - Design a flexible and efficient system for team members to utilize efficiently.
   - Monitor the efficiency and effectiveness of the system regularly.
   - Make improvements with minimal bureaucracy.
4. Acknowledge knowledge transfer ideas promptly:
   - Establish and enforce prompt response times.
   - Talk to team members in person when possible.
   - Avoid using impersonal form letters or emails.

CREATING A TEAM SUCCESSION PLAN

Change is a constant in a project team environment. People join and leave teams all the time. The scope, budget, requirements, and deadlines are altered continuously. Market conditions fluctuate, and clients alter their expectations. Project teams are vulnerable to these changes. Knowing the end goal, direction, and available resources for team projects and activities can help team members handle the uncertainty of frequent changes and avoid being distracted by the processes, people, and politics of the past. Planning for succession is another essential leadership function that anticipates required growth and development on teams to ensure their longevity and resiliency. Rod Landgraff, CEO, RALYE Enterprises, and leadership mentor, explains that

> "an enduring legacy of leadership is its succession planning and how it inspires others. It is carefully crafted, properly developed, and vibrant with relationships and best practices."*

A team succession plan is a powerful tool to keep a team grounded as members learn to work more productively to synchronize their knowledge, skills, and abilities as a cohesive unit. A team succession plan is a specialized document essential to the organizational succession planning process. It is usually initiated, approved, and endorsed by the board of directors, CEO, human resources department, and other senior management professionals. Some companies integrate the team succession plan into the human resource plan to ensure that it is strategically aligned with the organizational infrastructure. Those organizations and project sponsors that encourage or require team succession plans do so because they gain the same benefits as hierarchical organizations—retaining and promoting talented staff, minimizing expenses for recruiting and training new people, increasing job satisfaction, and being more competitive in the marketplace.

No team succession plan is like another. Each plan is the outcome of the unique vision, mission, and goals of the team and the knowledge, skills, and abilities that exist or may be developed on that team. Despite

---

* Rob Landgraff, RALYE Enterprises, interview, August 12, 2011.

individual differences in content and format, there are usually three categories addressed in a team succession plan:

1. *Knowledge transfer:* Relevant information shared by team members that enables them to attain performance goals more accurately, efficiently, and consistently. (Example: How will Team A acquire relevant software development knowledge from Team B for a new IT project?)
2. *Skill development:* Various levels of specific competencies demonstrated when applying knowledge to complete tasks successfully. (Example: High, moderate, or low skill in writing a team succession plan)
3. *Ability contribution:* Strengths or characteristics of general competencies. (Example: Ability to think strategically)

The first place to start when writing a team succession plan is to include the following information, but not necessarily in the same order.

Team Succession Plan Components

- Team name, description, purpose
- Key projects and priorities
- Team vision, mission, goal(s): short term (up to 2 years) and longer term (3 to 5 years)
- All or parts of the project charter and human resources plan (if applicable)
- All or parts of the project communications plan (if applicable)
- All or parts of the organizational succession plan (if applicable)
- Specific short-term and long-term needs the team will address and priorities

Target stakeholders affected (external to the team and/or to the organization):

- *Team members:* Names, titles, work status (full-time, part-time, contractual, work locations by office/country, job descriptions, project roles and responsibilities, multigenerational information (if available and appropriate)
- *Union requirements* (if appropriate)
- *Legal requirements* (if appropriate)

- *Team knowledge base:* Current and projected
- *Explicit:* Objective and measurable, such as technical data and project requirements
- *Tacit:* Interpretative and subjective related to categories such as: people, processes, technology, associative thinking, and emotional agility

Team skills:
- *Current level of proficiency,* such as basic-level software knowledge
- *Future level of proficiency,* such as all team members to complete the Master's Certificate in Project Management by the end of the next fiscal year

SUMMARY: KEY IDEAS

Team "Brain" of Knowledge

- Team knowledge transfer is very important to the development of project teams. The team "brain" of knowledge comes from the team members whose composite thinking has left- and right-brain components. "Brain drain" occurs when individual knowledge is not fully developed or transferred within the team.

Knowledge Transfer Guidelines

- Ensure that the action plan for team knowledge transfer supports the team vision, mission, and goals.
- Include an oral knowledge transfer segment with documentation at each team meeting.
- Schedule regular coaching and mentoring activities.

Knowledge Transfer Methods

- Create a policy for team knowledge transfer.
- Publicize a process for generating ideas.
- Develop a system for efficient record keeping.
- Acknowledge ideas for knowledge transfer promptly.

Creating a Team Succession Plan

A team succession plan is an important document that can help manage the team knowledge transfer process and avoid team "brain drain." No two team succession plans are identical, but there are usually three distinct categories:

1. Knowledge transfer: Relevant information shared by team members.
2. Skill development: Level of specific competency when applying knowledge.
3. Ability contribution: Strengths or characteristics of general competencies.

8

Leading Team Transformation

Patrick (New Manager, Information Systems): *"I know I was hired primarily to lead team transformation for the next three years. The challenge is where to start."*

Ben (Senior Director, Enterprise Management and Patrick's coach): *"Let me ask you two questions that can help you to focus: How would your clients describe your team at present, and how would you prefer your clients to describe your team three years from now?"*

Patrick: *"Our surveys indicate that our clients perceive our team as technically proficient but difficult to relate to interpersonally. Clients frequently use words such as 'too detailed,' 'bureaucratic,' and 'impersonal.' My vision for the team in the future is that clients will say consistently that the team 'designed, developed, and installed user-friendly software for them with a humane touch.'"*

Ben: *"So let's assume this idea represents the team vision. What changes do you think are needed to achieve that vision?"*

Patrick: *"As a team, we need to eliminate unnecessary administrative tasks and paperwork, speak to our clients using nontechnical language, respond to their questions quickly and nondefensively, and simplify our processes so they are easy for clients to implement. We have to really believe that the customer comes first."*

Ben: *"So I think we now know where to start!"*

Patrick: *"With these action steps?"*

Ben: *"No. First we need to finalize the team vision statement so you can communicate it clearly and frequently to the team and gain their awareness, understanding, commitment, and support. Without a vision for the team, there can be no transformation."*

TRANSFORMING TEAMS AT A PROJECT LEVEL

There is a lot of talk today at the CEO level about team transformation. But what does this look like at the project level from the perspective of most project managers and business analysts who are assigned responsibility to make it happen? In the above dialogue, Patrick's response to his mandated role as a change leader offers a glimpse of how difficult it is in a project environment for a manager to bring about transformation in the future when he feels so much pressure to take action immediately in the present. At the very least, project professionals face continuous changes in scope, requirements, deadlines, stakeholders, resources, budgets, regulations, customer needs, and marketplace trends. They also face tremendous pressure from the senior ranks to fix immediate problems that cannot be rectified without having a clear vision for what the end results should look like. They can be overwhelmed, not knowing where to start, as in Patrick's case.

It is often tempting for project professionals in Patrick's position, feeling pressured by time to change a team culture quickly, to take action immediately without doing much or any planning. They know they have to achieve certain performance goals within a certain time frame, all too often with less time, money, and resources than required to do the job effectively. Ben, his coach, cautions Patrick that identifying and communicating a vision for the transformation is the first step. Unless Patrick consistently communicates the vision to team members, he will not be able to help them evolve from subject matter experts to customer-oriented service providers.

LEADING TRANSFORMATION: WHAT IS REQUIRED?

When asked to articulate his own vision for the team, Patrick anticipated that his team would need to evolve from being driven by technology and bureaucracy to becoming more customer centric in attitude, relationships, and performance. The odds against his success cannot be over-estimated. The intent of transformation is to change a form or substance, appearance, character, or disposition. When a team is transformed, the outward manifestation of the changes is usually seen last. The team's character and disposition, essentially the internal core of the team, has to change from the inside before any changes can be noticed from the outside. To modify the collective values, assumptions, and beliefs that affect how team members think, feel, and act is a tremendous undertaking for anyone responsible for transforming teams.

The hardest and most time-consuming part of the transformation process is preparing the team to manage the stressors related to it. Pushing the team to act before members are ready can end up with what looks like transformation, but is actually just a temporary change. In a fast-paced work environment where team members are pressured to fulfill deliverables without necessarily knowing or committing to the team vision, little if any progress to achieve transformation is likely. When individuals adjust their schedules, work output, and knowledge base, they can accomplish change efficiently. But these modifications are not enough to actually transform them or their team. When a team is transformed, it experiences major shifts beyond daily changes. Unless team members comprehend, appreciate, and accept the vision emotionally as well as professionally, they will not be sufficiently motivated to exert the effort and take the risks necessary for the transformation to succeed.

Supporting the Vision

To become truly transformed, individuals and teams need to have strong leaders with a clear vision for the future, leaders who foster as well as model the following attitudes and behaviors:

- A management support system that encourages transformation despite the risks
- A forward-looking mindset that lets go of the past and embraces the present and future
- A clear understanding of what the transformation entails and why it is planned
- The necessary knowledge and understanding to make a commitment to new attitudes and behaviors required to achieve the team vision
- Believing and committing to the changes personally and professionally
- Learning and applying new best practices that embody the vision
- Supporting and encouraging others to fulfill the vision
- Building a collaborative team "community" based on mutual trust and continuous improvement

Communicating the Team Vision

It takes time for team members to internalize a vision so they believe in it emotionally as well as understand it intellectually. So it is vital to publicize the vision continuously—before, during, and after the transformation. The vision has more impact when it is communicated to the team using many different media, including orally, email, internal websites, and on printed posters in meeting rooms, in the cafeteria, and anywhere else where members visit. In addition to helping team members model the vision, leaders need to help them develop the skills necessary for making changes and managing the related stressors proactively. The following twelve steps are recommended for team leaders to follow to be successful.

Focusing Teams on the Vision

1. *Seeing, hearing, appreciating, and applying the team vision:* The team needs to see, hear, and apply the team vision regularly so it becomes a regular part of routine conversations and activities. It is not enough to mention it once or occasionally. Some organizations post both the corporate and team vision statements in meeting areas and on internal documents to ensure that they are communicating to all team members continuously and consistently. Other organizations even have posters in key areas, such as the customer lobby, meeting rooms, elevators, bathrooms, and cafeteria.

2. *Modeling the vision:* It is essential that senior executive leaders model the vision so they can build a trusting emotional climate in the organization. Team members expect their senior leaders to practice what they preach.

3. *Explaining what changes need to be made and why:* It is natural for team members to resist changing their attitudes and behaviors. If they understand the benefits, then they are more likely to commit to and carry out what is required to achieve the intended transformation.

4. *Moving forward from the past emotionally and intellectually:* Team members can find it difficult to let go of the past, especially if dwelling on it becomes a habit. They need to know operating norms for what new behaviors they are expected to demonstrate, and play an active role in being responsible and accountable. Coaching and mentoring can also play a vital role to provide the appropriate support to both the leader and team members.

5. *Demonstrating team commitment to the vision:* Introducing new processes and clear performance standards for the team to achieve the vision collectively is akin to the glue that helps individual substances stick together. Evaluating progress toward achieving the vision can also be a unifying experience for the team during the time that it evolves into its new transformational state.

6. *Engaging members in discussions about the team charter:* When team members feel connected to the team charter, they also play a fundamental role in the team's transformation. Because the team charter documents the team's mission, aims, principles, function, membership, and relevant project requirements, keeping it top of mind for all team members helps build their commitment to the transformational vision that the charter supports.

7. *Developing team knowledge and skills to make the changes:* By acquiring information and skills to make the necessary changes, the team will be more prepared to assume new roles and responsibilities as part of the transformation. Knowledge development and transfer among members is vital for the team's success in adapting to a future state of thinking, interacting, and performing.

8. *Implementing ideas for change:* Seeing their ideas and efforts materialize as a result of team planning can be a very satisfying experience for team members. Following through on promises and fine-tuning new processes can help the team become more creative, innovative, and adaptive, so they are better prepared for the change.

9. *Discussing team challenges and progress:* Ensuring that the team has frequent opportunities to discuss challenges and evaluate progress toward the transformational vision and team charter mission based on specific measurement standards will both motivate and guide the team as it progresses.

10. *Rediscovering the vision:* Finding new ways to expand, explore, execute, and redefine how to apply the vision in their daily activities and planning processes will motivate team members by giving them a voice to contribute their input for the future.

11. *Celebrating team milestones:* Regularly celebrating small successes will keep the team informed, motivated, and engaged for increased individual and collective accountability. Small steps of change in their mindset and actions can lead the way to the right path to complete the journey of transformation.

12. *Fostering a collaborative "community" mindset:* Collaborating as a community of individuals connected by a common vision is an ideal way to inspire the team. As team members find new ways to involve each other in collaborating on problem solving, decision making, and innovation, they will form a stronger bond that will help them manage obstacles in unity.

Benefits of a Transformational Team

A transformational team makes substantial changes in thinking, responding, and acting (Figure 8.1).

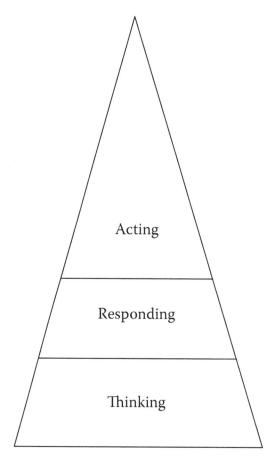

FIGURE 8.1
Three levels of team transformation.

Transformational teams are necessary for organizations to remain competitive in an increasingly customer-focused marketplace. Project teams that keep in touch with the customer experiences of their internal and external stakeholders generally increase their potential to develop loyal customer "advocates" and retain them longer. For project stakeholders, the customer experience is more "emotional" and less "rational" than most will admit readily. Their memories of interactions with the team have tremendous staying power with strong positive or negative associations, depending on how they felt the team dealt with their needs. Stakeholders can formulate emotional, visual, and experiential associations that are not captured in surveys or are overlooked in customer interactions. These insights provide valuable information for continuous improvements to the team's culture, processes, technology, and policies.

Drawbacks for Teams Undergoing Transformation

A team undergoing transformation is susceptible to many distractions from project work. First, team members managing a demanding workload with short-term deadlines may find it difficult to invest time and energy to change their mindset, habits, processes, methods, job priorities, and skills. Making changes is difficult and threatening to many team leaders and members. Although the benefits of developing a transformational team are visible once the changes are complete, getting there is not guaranteed. Some people will avoid change altogether because they want to remain in the past or the present. Others will deny it due to discomfort or disbelief. Some individuals will resent change, refuse to adapt, and leave the team and organization. Others will tolerate change with indifference and lose their career passion. Those individuals who do make an effort to adapt cannot do it by themselves; they need the direction and support of a strong leader.

Team Skills Needed for Transformation

To guide teams to achieve true transformation, leaders need to follow a plan of action for helping the team develop a unique set of skills that are especially useful during times of uncertainty and change. The following are eight essential skills that differentiate visionary leaders and their teams from others not capable of moving beyond the status quo:

1. *Tolerance of ambiguity:* The mental and emotional abilities to address ambiguity without frustration or confusion are essential skills for managing change. Team members who tolerate and even appreciate ambiguity tend to visualize solutions and options that are more innovative and profitable. They flex their creativity to see the bigger picture when challenged by ambiguous information or situations. Individuals and teams that are more comfortable with information and processes that are not ambiguous struggle during times of change because of their inability to cope with uncertainty.

2. *Flexible thinking and problem-solving skills:* Teams that are able to undergo a transformation exhibit a variety of thinking styles, including: strategic planning, analytical reasoning, intuitive insights, innovative capabilities, administrative know-how, and tactical abilities. They are more likely to capitalize on whole-brain thinking—using both their left-brain (logical, sequential, linear reasoning) and right-brain (intuitive, spontaneous, and nonlinear) thinking to consider all possible options to problems and opportunities. The result is typically sound problem solving based on the best possible options for the future.

3. *Expertise influencing others at all levels:* The skill to influence others, regardless of authority level, is a key ingredient for change adaptation. Being able to influence others to get things done is a fundamental skill for increased productivity and career resiliency, especially when in the midst of changing job scope, areas of responsibility, and work processes.

4. *Emotional intelligence:* Team members who exhibit emotional intelligence are able to establish trust and collaboration under even the most trying of circumstances. Emotional intelligence skills that are especially useful during times of transition and transformation include self-awareness, empathy, self-management of conflict and stress responses, and optimism in the face of adversity. Instead of giving up or getting even, team members possessing these aspects of emotional resiliency are well prepared to cope with the uncertainty of what the future brings in a transformational culture.

5. *Career resiliency:* Resiliency is a state of thinking and acting that enables one to bounce back successfully from career-related disappointments, challenges, setbacks, and difficult situations. Project professionals exhibiting career resiliency are proactive about developing portable skills they can use in their future that will enable

them to readily adapt to workplace changes. These individuals thrive on teams undergoing transformation because they tend to manage well the stress of change, and are willing to invest time and energy developing new skills.

6. *Calculated risk-taking:* Typically, in a change-averse project environment, teams are required to follow established guidelines and processes to reduce financial, legal, operational, and project-related risks. In contrast, calculated risk-taking is a necessity to achieve transformation to ensure that the team does not miss significant opportunities for change, innovation, growth, and vision fulfillment. Transformational leaders recognize that they need to build a culture that encourages team members to take risks at times, be accountable for the consequences, and focus on the lessons learned instead of mistakes for self-growth.

7. *Intercultural communications competence:* Communicating appropriately with diverse cultures is a prerequisite for teams to succeed in transformations. Conveying clear messages to multicultural team members helps foster collaborative partnerships that are enriched by different cultural perspectives. Team members demonstrating intercultural communications competence understand how to convey messages with impact. They know how to communicate effectively to *low-context* cultures that value individuality, order, consistency, hierarchical decision making, and written rules. They can also demonstrate equal confidence and competence when communicating to *high-context* cultures that embrace collectivism, spontaneity, decentralized decision making, trust, and oral traditions.

8. *Facilitating knowledge exchange:* Team members need to develop effective facilitation skills so they can stimulate others to conduct meaningful dialogues that result in effective knowledge exchange. Understanding how diverse individuals process information fosters more efficient conversations by focusing on ground rules, norms for behavior, and specific processes for discussion, disagreement, debate, and decision making.

Leading Team Transformation: Best Practices

Transformational leaders add value to teams by encouraging them to challenge the status quo when necessary and appropriate to support the vision. These leaders facilitate engagement within their teams by inspiring commitment and fostering innovation and collaborative decision making. Their aim is to promote growth in their teams, both individually and collectively, based on self-awareness and discovery, as well as creative problem solving with others. They lead primarily through collaboration and trust to engage others to make a commitment to change attitudes and behaviors through innovation and risk-taking when necessary. They participate in continuous improvement for themselves and their team, especially to identify and remedy knowledge and learning gaps that can interfere with achieving the vision.

Transformational leaders typically follow these best practices to support the vision for the team:

- Participative (versus bureaucratic) decision making
- Power *with* people instead of *over* people
- Consensual group problem solving
- Adding value through innovative practices
- Shared goal setting
- Shared "leadership"
- Delegating "power" to others
- Actively seeking different interpretations and approaches
- Involving team members in self-governance
- Public recognition of individual and group efforts
- Conducting surveys to identify levels of engagement among team members and stakeholders and seeking new ideas to support the vision
- Leading with influence and charisma (versus formal authority)
- Creating and implementing coaching and mentoring training for all team members on an ongoing basis
- Implementing continuous improvement opportunities for innovation in support of the team vision

Why Teams Lose Their Transformative Powers

In a project environment where so much emphasis is placed on the bottom line, it is challenging for a team to focus on a vision long enough to achieve transformation. When teams achieve change, they need strong leadership support and encouragement to continue the momentum or the team risks losing its transformative powers. Key reasons why teams lose their capacity for change include

1. *Absentee leadership*: When visionary team leaders do not take an active role in developing the team to manage change, its members can lose interest in the team's progress and become preoccupied with their own self-interests.

2. *No visionary focus*: Without constant communications about the vision, the team loses focus on its unifying purpose as a collective unit and loses its momentum for transformation.

3. *Low commitment*: If team members have a low commitment to the vision or the changes required to achieve that vision, the team's potential to achieve the transformation is limited.

4. *No formalized processes*: Lacking ground rules, norms, and other formalized processes for discussion, disagreement, debate, and decision making can leave the team vulnerable to regressing to storming and forming behaviors.

5. *Poor conflict management*: An absence or abundance of conflict within the team can distract members' attention from the vision for the future to survival tactics for the present.

6. *Lack of succession planning*: The lack of a team succession plan can make it difficult to continue transformational efforts if the visionary leader leaves.

7. *Vision misalignment*: If the team vision is not aligned with the organizational vision, there is the risk that the team will not have sufficient support to achieve its vision for change.

8. *Lack of innovation*: The inability to create innovative ideas that appeal to stakeholders and customers can cause teams to fail in their transformational efforts. It is important that the organization minimizes any unnecessary bureaucracy that can potentially interfere with team processes to foster innovation and creative thinking.

SUMMARY: KEY IDEAS

Transforming Teams: Best Practices

Transformational leaders add value to teams by encouraging them to challenge the status quo when appropriate to support the vision. They lead primarily through collaboration and trust to engage others to make a commitment to change attitudes and behaviors through innovation and risk-taking when necessary. They participate in continuous improvement for themselves and their team, especially to identify and remedy knowledge and learning gaps that can potentially interfere with supporting the vision.

A clear vision that all team members understand and believe in is essential for transforming teams. There are twelve steps required for leaders to achieve transformation within their teams:

1. Seeing, hearing, and applying the vision in routine team conversations and activities
2. Modeling the vision from the senior executive level downward
3. Explaining what changes need to be made and why
4. Moving forward from the past, both emotionally and intellectually
5. Demonstrating team commitment to the vision by introducing new processes and performance standards
6. Involving team members in creating and updating the team charter
7. Developing team knowledge and skills to make the changes
8. Implementing ideas for change for innovation and adaptation
9. Discussing team challenges and progress regularly with the team
10. Rediscovering the vision by finding new ways to expand, explore, execute, and redefine it
11. Celebrating team milestones as small successes occur
12. Fostering a collaborative "community" mindset

9

Future of Teams

Marilyn (project manager with extensive team development experience):
"Now that I have extensive team development experience, I am wondering what job opportunities I can expect in the next twenty years before I retire."

Winston (business analyst with some team leadership experience): *"Your guess is as good as mine. I expect companies to contract team developers with business management experience to develop their virtual teams. I predict that the project teams of the future will be expanded to include customers, vendors, and other business partners with global management expertise."*

Marilyn: *"That's very likely; I am observing this trend in a few client organizations we serve. It is interesting that you mention the possibility of contracts for more specialized team developers to work for particular PM and BA projects. Maybe you should consider going back to school for an MBA or a business-related certificate to upgrade your BA certification."*

Winston: *"Yes, I will consider taking courses in business management and interpersonal communications, especially if the organization pays for it. I can certainly imagine working as a contract "leader" for virtual teams based from a home office and using my business analyst expertise when required."*

Marilyn: *"Well, this is all speculation. For those of us interested in the future of team planning in a project environment, it will be an interesting ride for the next few decades, for sure."*

NECESSITY FOR TEAM DEVELOPMENT PLANNING

Many team development specialists are hopeful that in the next few decades, CEOs and their senior management team will become more enlightened about the strategic discipline of "team development" and will no longer confuse it with the more tactical aspects of "team building." From a business management perspective, all teams—co-located, virtual, and global—will be needed more than ever for greater project agility, customer responsiveness, and innovation. Those individuals with expertise developing teams, including Marilyn and Winston in the opening dialogue, can make a unique contribution that will help organizations become more productive, innovative, and profitable in the years ahead.

FROM "SOFT" TO "ESSENTIAL"

Team development in a project environment is becoming a priority to keep organizations more competitive in the marketplace. Teams, rather than individuals, will be relied upon more than ever to create, deliver, and support products and services that are both innovative and profitable. An organization's capacity to maximize its team output will set it apart from its competitors and ensure its longevity.

Team development specialist Patrick Lencioni emphasizes the "untapped" nature of teamwork by saying,

> "...in this day and age of informational ubiquity and nanosecond change, teamwork remains the one sustainable competitive advantage that has been largely untapped. In the course of my career as a consultant to executives and their teams, I can say confidently that teamwork is almost always lacking in organizations that fail, and often present within those that succeed."[*]

As team productivity becomes more essential, organizations are expected to invest more in outsourcing leadership specialists in team development. The increased acceptance of team development as a credible professional

---

[*] Lencioni, Patrick. *Overcoming the Five Dysfunctions of a Team: A Field Guide,* San Francisco, CA: Jossey-Bass, 2005, p. 3.

specialty with its own comprehensive knowledge base should help to distinguish it from the general activity of "team building." Despite the fact that team effectiveness is difficult to measure, a solid team development plan—with quantitative as well as qualitative performance criteria—makes it possible to track progress and ensure adequate returns on this investment. Organizations will rely on project leaders to contribute the following skills to safeguard the productivity and profitability of their teams:

- Write comprehensive team development plans that are strategically aligned with organizational goals.
- Provide training, coaching, and mentoring expertise to develop teams into high-performing units faster.
- Facilitate meetings, especially pertaining to creative problem solving, between team members and business partners.
- Advise senior management on how to reinforce the team development at all levels of the organization.

As a consequence of organizations relying more heavily on team development expertise as an essential business management skill, project managers (PMs) and business analysts (BAs) will be required to expand their knowledge beyond technical expertise to include business management and team development to qualify for project leadership positions.

In the next two decades, team leaders could be responsible for achieving specific performance goals for each stage of the team's development by demonstrating advanced-level knowledge and competency in the following essential skills, which will probably not be considered "soft skills" anymore:

- Techniques for assertiveness and diplomacy
- Methodologies for creative thinking and problem solving
- Strategic and tactical training in conflict resolution
- Demonstrated negotiation and influencing skills
- Certification in group processes for collaboration
- Core business management knowledge from a CEO, sponsor, or senior management perspective
- Expertise in writing strategies and objectives for team development
- Intercultural competency in oral and written communications
- Knowledge of the psychology and group dynamics of teams

CHANGES IN PROJECT TEAM MEMBERSHIP

As project teams become a more valued resource, their composition will likely change to include customers, business partners, vendors, and other key stakeholders in cross-functional relationships with project specialists. For these team members to work together effectively, they will need a common business management language that is broader than the technical jargon and methodologies of PMs and BAs. Managing information transfer in a fast-paced team environment among technical and non-technical professionals will make teamwork more challenging than ever before. Teams will need more flexibility and resiliency to remain competitive in the marketplace and responsive to customer needs.

Keeping up with these changes will demand new competencies to cope effectively, according to an IBM executive study conducted in 2010 and based on face-to-face conversations with more than 1,541 senior private- and public-sector leaders representing more than 700 organizations of various sizes in 61 countries[*]. In this groundbreaking research, the ability to communicate interculturally, intergenerationally, and in a variety of styles was considered necessary for managing the complexities that organizations will face in the future[†].

Survey respondents also emphasized the growing need for team members to demonstrate "collective intelligence" through more collaboration on global teams, especially using virtual media. Improving "cross-functional effectiveness by providing an on-line platform for virtual team collaboration" was identified as the primary means to combine global and local talent[‡].

What is surprising about the IBM research study is that it identifies a new paradigm for leadership as a continuous creative process, instead of accessing creative resources only when required. This type of leadership is described in the research as one that will be needed both strategically, in terms of the big picture and overall vision, as well as tactically to improve processes, procedures, and daily tasks continuously[§]. The study describes this approach as embracing ambiguity and taking risks that disrupt the

---

[*] "Working Beyond Borders. Insights from the Global Chief Human Resource Officer Study," IBM Corporation, 2010. Accessed February 4, 2012. <http://www-935.ibm.com/services/c-suite/chro/study.html>.

[†] Ibid., p. 24, 43–51, 37.

[‡] Ibid., p. 24, 43–51, 37.

[§] Ibid., p. 24, 43–51, 37.

legacy of more tried-and-true business models and management styles. The emphasis on developing what the IBM study calls "creative leadership" is based on the respondents' input that simplifying processes whenever possible and honoring customers above all else to be in sync with their needs will enable organizations to profit from the information explosion from technology and social media. The ability of teams to change their structures to "align talent in new business areas" was stressed as one of the most pressing needs in the future[*].

The tremendous potential of this type of creative leadership to shape the future development of teams is an exciting prospect for team development specialists. They will be challenged to transform teams to become more proficient in the following additional ways:

1. *Developing self-reliance:* The opportunity to transform a team from following rules and procedures without questioning them to challenging existing processes with self-reliance.
2. *Managing ambiguity:* The challenge of coaching and mentoring PMs and BAs to manage ambiguous information with more comfort and confidence.
3. *Coaching and mentoring:* The unique experience of coaching and mentoring customers, vendors, business partners, and colleagues as integral members of the project team.
4. *Providing mediation:* The expanded network of team partners will require effective mediation skills to prevent, address, and resolve conflicts that will inevitably arise due to diverse perspectives and priorities.
5. *Contributing business management expertise:* The expanded role of focusing the team's attention on the broader scope of business management will offer added value and expertise beyond the technical aspects of project management and business analysis.
6. *Emphasizing strategic alignment:* The visionary approach of ensuring that the team's goals are aligned with the goals of the business will encourage team members to think more strategically.
7. *Promoting creativity:* The necessity for continuously reinventing processes and procedures will require team developers to coach and mentor team members on creative approaches that use both intuitive, right-brain and logical, left-brain thinking approaches.

---

[*] Ibid., p. 24, 43–51, 37.

8. *Encouraging personal interaction:* Although social media usage will undoubtedly increase, the team will still need more planned interactions that encourage personal relationship building to help the team progress in its life cycle.

9. *Ensuring succession planning:* Succession planning will require more attention than ever before to ensure a career path that retains high-potential employees who demonstrate effective business management skills.

10. *Improving intercultural communications:* Educating team members about how to communicate more effectively globally with diverse cultures will help to build team relationships and avoid misunderstandings that can cause errors and delays on projects.

TRENDS FOR PMS AND BAS

From Project Specialists to Business Generalists

As more CEOs, senior managers, and sponsors stress the development of general business management skills for all the team members on a project, PMs and BAs interested in team leadership positions will be tasked in the next few decades to become business generalists as well as project specialists. They will need more than subject matter expertise to compete in the job market. Those individuals capable of communicating and transforming the organization's business vision, mission, and goals into marketable products and services will offer added value and earn unique opportunities for career advancement.

From Office to Home

It is probable that due to advances in technology and cost savings, a greater number of team members will be working from home and interacting with each other more frequently in a virtual setting. Daniel Arbour, manager for a global retailer, predicts that,

> "In the next twenty years, the landscape of the project team will be defined by the communication tools at their disposal. These tools will be tangible and intangible assets available to each team member and project manager.

Physical work environments will be transformed by technologies at our disposal. We will see the expansion of Web method skills that allow PMs and BAs to contact their teams throughout the globe. Faster Internet bandwidth and computing speed will result in significantly less drag and increased data processing power, enabling virtual teams to prove themselves more effective than today's virtual teams. These new realities will allow updated streaming audio and visual tools to project the physical realm through a virtual portal."[*]

Educating, inspiring, and influencing team stakeholders will play a more important role as information dissemination becomes quicker and easier. Instead of spending meeting time updating team members about their respective project responsibilities, PMs and BAs will need to coach and educate team members to assume the same or similar roles in support of the team's goals through cultural adaptation. Daniel Arbour explains that,

"as a result of globally located and specialized team members, project managers and project team members will need to ensure they understand cultural and religious holidays. PMs will need to manage project schedules and practice cultural norms."[†]

From Left Brain to Whole Brain

Those PMs and BAs who demonstrate whole brain capabilities will be more upwardly mobile in an increasingly competitive workplace where creativity will become more valued as an essential skill. Although left-brain approaches, including sequential thinking, root-cause analysis, analytical reasoning, and numerical computation, will continue to be important, right-brain methods, including free association, intuitive analysis, mind mapping, and creative benchmarking, will become essential for initiating and executing ideas for continuous improvement and innovation.

Becoming More Entrepreneurial

It is expected that in the upcoming decades, organizations will promote more risk-taking and decision making among PMs and BAs. Companies

---

[*] Daniel Arbour, B. Comm., Int. Mgmt. Manager, Retail Pricing and Demand Management Canada, Shell Canada Limited, Toronto, Ontario, Canada.

[†] Ibid.

will need to adapt new technologies and processes quickly to meet constantly changing customer requirements. Organizations will promote project professionals with an entrepreneurial mindset capable of challenging the status quo assertively and influencing team members and other stakeholders successfully to make systems and processes increasingly agile.

Becoming Relationship Managers

Teams of the future will have expanded memberships with clients, customers, vendors, and other business partners. Managing these relationships productively will become an integral part of the role for PMs and BAs. More team time will be spent on communications to build rapport, develop a common language using shared terminology, gain buy-in and commitment, and resolve disagreements, disputes, and conflicts. Therefore, appealing to others' motivations by engaging them in collaborative discussions to assess risks, problems, and opportunities will become more of a core requirement for PMs and BAs. As a result, establishing good public relations with others outside the team structure will become more of an organizational priority for project professionals. Project team developers will be tasked to identify and promote "high potential" individuals with superior communications skills.

Coaching Peers

Organizations will require newcomers with differing perspectives to add vitality to their projects while also adapting quickly to project requirements. These newcomers could be recent graduates or co-operative students from a university, college, or technical school, or individuals from another department within the organization. A cost-effective way to accomplish this goal is to entrust PMs and BAs to coach these new peers in a collaborative and noncompetitive manner. In return, the coaches will gain essential business management expertise.

Although peer coaching will be valued more by Generation Y and Generation Z team members, they will have to manage a few drawbacks. First, peers may lack adequate professional training or experience to be effective in coaching colleagues with different learning styles. Second, peers might not feel comfortable sharing knowledge and tips with others, especially a colleague with equal authority or an individual who is not a direct report. Third, if the coach is more interested in delegating than in coaching, tension and conflict could arise within the team.

Nonetheless, the team benefit of peer coaching for project professionals and their organizations is that comprehensive knowledge transfer will occur in four key areas:

1. Work style approaches
2. Academic training
3. Work experience
4. Personal and professional interests

Managing Upward

Managing expectations and "selling" ideas upward to sponsors, senior managers, CEOs, and boards of directors will also become more highly valued skills for BAs and PMs. The ability to reframe project details into selling points that align strategically with the corporate vision, business goals, and objectives will enable project professionals to build important alliances necessary for goal setting, resource allocation, and productivity gains. Managing upward can expand team access to valuable business information affecting projects, reduce unnecessary time waiting for approvals, and increase team ownership and pride through better sponsorship support. Project professionals with the skill to manage upward will acquire more visibility, credibility, and support for their teams, plus the added benefit of unique career advancement opportunities for themselves.

Demonstrating Career Resiliency

Organizations will expect project team members to be self-reliant and proficient in handling obstacles, setbacks, unexpected crises, ambiguity, and new roles. Demonstrating resourcefulness utilizing technology for social networking, project collaboration, and intercultural communications will also become competitive skills for professionals seeking upward mobility quickly. Those individuals with the energy and longevity to adapt proactively to team challenges will be considered greater assets to teams and "high potentials" for upward mobility in the organizations that employ them.

SUMMARY: KEY IDEAS

Future of Team Development Planning

From a business management perspective, organizations will value team development more than ever before in the next two decades. Executives will expect greater project agility, customer responsiveness, innovation, and adaptation in a competitive global marketplace. Organizations will invest in team development based on the following priorities:

- Project leadership utilizing general business management and strategic development competencies
- Multigenerational and intercultural communications fluency for effective knowledge transfer
- Project teams will be expanded to include customers, business partners, and vendors along with PMs and BAs
- Team members coaching and mentoring each other, especially when facing ambiguity, taking risks, anticipating customer needs, and managing complex information
- Keeping up with the pace of change, especially the need to build operating dexterity, re-invent customer relationships, and embody creative leadership
- Communicating both globally and locally to manage the complexities of change

CEOs will expect PMs and BAs to become proficient in essential skills that will no longer be viewed as "soft":

- Assertiveness and diplomacy
- Creative thinking and problem solving
- Conflict resolution
- Self-awareness and self-management of reactions
- Certification for collaborative group processes
- Core business management knowledge
- Strategic writing expertise
- Intercultural competence in oral and written communications
- Knowledge of team psychology and group dynamics

Appendix

A.1 PM AND BA TEAM PLANNING COMPETENCY ASSESSMENT

TEMPLATE OVERVIEW	TEMPLATE PREPARATION	DATE
Evaluate team planning readiness based on three dimensions: (1) Vision, (2) Methodology, and (3) Observation Capabilities	**Prepared By:**	
	Approved By:	

TEAM NAME	
TEAM PROJECT(S)	
TEAM COMPOSITION	
Number of Team Members	_____Full-time + _____Part-Time + _____Other = _____Total Other (Please specify): _____
Team Location	☐ All Virtual ☐ All In-Person ☐ Combination of the two
Team Duration (includes all current members)	☐ Less Than 1 Year ☐ 1–3 Years ☐ 4–6 Years ☐ 7+ Years

TEAM ASSIGNMENT: OVERVIEW	
Your Authority Level over Team Members	☐ Formal Authority ☐ Responsibility Without Authority
Your Position within the Team	☐ Team Leader ☐ Sponsor ☐ Project Leader ☐ Other (Please specify: _____)

SKILL COMPETENCY ASSESSMENT					
COMPETENCY 1: VISION	**1 = WEAK - - - 5 = STRONG**				
I know how to write a team vision statement	☐	☐	☐	☐	☐
I know the vision for our organization	☐	☐	☐	☐	☐
I have a clear vision of my future role as a team leader	☐	☐	☐	☐	☐
I have a clear vision of my team's future state	☐	☐	☐	☐	☐
I communicate the team vision to my team regularly	☐	☐	☐	☐	☐

SKILL COMPETENCY ASSESSMENT					
COMPETENCY 2: METHODOLOGY	**1 = WEAK - - - 5 = STRONG**				
I use deliberate processes for team knowledge transfer	☐	☐	☐	☐	☐
I document methods for team discussion, agreement, and disagreement	☐	☐	☐	☐	☐
I am systematic about how I set expectations for my team	☐	☐	☐	☐	☐
I use a clear process to communicate the team vision	☐	☐	☐	☐	☐
I am effective in planning for knowledge transfer on my team	☐	☐	☐	☐	☐
I consistently promote and publicize my team to other teams within the organization	☐	☐	☐	☐	☐
COMPETENCY 3: OBSERVATION CAPABILITIES	**1 = WEAK - - - 5 = STRONG**				
I am very observant of team member proxemics (physical distances)	☐	☐	☐	☐	☐
I am especially observant of vocalics (vocal delivery and tone) at team meetings	☐	☐	☐	☐	☐
I know the difference between "high" and "low" contact team cultures	☐	☐	☐	☐	☐
I make a conscious effort to observe the "individualism" and "collectivism" of team members	☐	☐	☐	☐	☐
I communicate the team vision to my team regularly	☐	☐	☐	☐	☐
I am always seeking opportunities to observe the team's emotional intelligence (EQ)	☐	☐	☐	☐	☐

OVERALL – GENERAL COMMENTS	
Most proficient of the 3 categories:	**Key Behavior or Strength:**
Least proficient of the 3 categories:	**Key Behavior to Improve:**

A.2 OBSERVING TEAM BEHAVIORS: CHECKLIST

TEMPLATE OVERVIEW	TEMPLATE PREPARATION	DATE
Identify behaviors to observe to determine interpersonal effectiveness within the team.	Prepared By:	
	Approved By:	

TEAM NAME	
TEAM PROJECT(S)	

Team Behaviors	Observation Trends	General Notes
Proxemics: Level of comfort regarding the physical distance between team members	Average distance between people	
	Average distance between workspaces	
Vocalics: Vocal delivery, including tone	High vocal variety	
	Low vocal variety or monotone	
	Dysfunctional behaviors such as sarcastic tone	
	Use of paralanguage (uh, huh, um)	
Context: High or Low?	Low: Reliance on rules, regulations, and written documentation	
	High: Reliance on rituals, spontaneity, and undocumented approaches	
Tolerance of Ambiguity: How comfortable are team members with ambiguous information?	Low: Prefer tangible and consistent data	
	High: Able to deal well with uncertainty	

Team Behaviors	Observation Trends	General Notes
IQ: Intellectual intelligence	Level of technical skill proficiencies as PMs and BAs	
	Level of logical reasoning, abstract thinking, verbal and mathematical abilities	
EQ: Emotional intelligence	Self-management of stress, awareness of styles, emotional resiliency, intuition, assertiveness, conflict resolution	
	Level of social intelligence, especially during tension and conflict	
Contact: High or Low?	High: Maximum physical contact, including tendencies to shake hands and hug	
	Low: Minimal physical contact, including tendencies not to shake hands or touch	
Chronemics: Monochronic or Polychronic?	Monochronic: Time is not to be wasted: "Be on time"	
	Polychronic: Time flows: "We'll get there when we get there"	
Identity: Individualism or Collectivism?	Individualism: Team members prefer to work alone and make decisions separately	
	Collectivism: Team members prefer to work together and make decisions as a unit	
Attitudes toward Authority: High or Low Trust?	High Trust: Respect for authority figures and titles	
	Low Trust: Distrust for authority figures and job titles	

A.3 TEAM CONFLICT OBSERVATION GUIDE

TEMPLATE OVERVIEW	TEMPLATE PREPARATION	DATE
Identify what clues to observe at each conflict level and acquire leadership tips for effective conflict resolution.	Prepared By:	
	Approved By:	

CONFLICT LEVEL	TEAM STAGE(S) MOST LIKELY TO OCCUR	SYMPTOMS	ROOT CAUSES	LEADERSHIP TIPS	NOTES
Hidden	Forming Storming	• Minimal clues—facial expression or negative body language can occur • Silence, even when asked for input • What else? _____ • •	• Over-use of consensus • Unresolved interpersonal differences • No processes to address conflicts proactively • Defensive reactions, especially non-assertive or passive-aggressive • Fear of reprimand or negative consequences • What else? _____ • •	• Conduct individual interviews to ask questions to understand root causes • Empathize, don't criticize • Introduce a process the team can use to address concerns in a non-blaming way and in a safe environment	

Emerging	Storming	• Subtle vocal comments of disagreement • Negative facial expressions and body language • Gossiping • Blaming • Avoidance • Seeking alliances against the other party • Cliques • Visible discomfort • What else? _____ • • •	• Lack of self-control over conflict reactions • Blaming the person instead of the problem • Ongoing negativity • Lack of conflict management training and team processes to address issues • No ground rules for team member interaction • What else? _____ • • •	• Establish ground rules for behavioral norms and enforce them • Coach each team member on the self-management of conflict reactions • Neutralize the emerging conflict by refocusing on the goals or issues to be addressed • Introduce diplomatic and neutral language to help with emotional detachment for team communications to be in the "aim frame" instead of the "blame frame"
Active Conflict	Storming Norming Performing	• Outbursts • Yelling • Aggression • Fight-or-flight reactions that are easy to observe • Highly vocalized debate or discussion • Others observe, avoid or get involved, depending on their views of the people, the topic, and their conflict responses • What else? _____ • • •	• Underlying issues have not yet been addressed, and they can escalate upward in the organization • Lack of assertive communications • Fear of conflict has delayed the issues from being resolved earlier • Inadequate conflict resolution processes exist within the team • What else? _____ • • •	• Isolate the individuals involved if they are in a public setting • Identify a mutual goal to get agreement from all parties involved • Establish and enforce general rules for subsequent discussions • Interview each party separately to identify symptoms and issues • Refocus the team on business issues, next steps, and lessons learned • Don't take sides • Appoint a neutral, independent mediator if necessary

continued

CONFLICT LEVEL	TEAM STAGE(S) MOST LIKELY TO OCCUR	SYMPTOMS	ROOT CAUSES	LEADERSHIP TIPS	NOTES

Aftermath	Storming (slowest time to recover)
	
	Norming (moderate time to recover)
	
	Performing (fastest time to recover)
		• Preoccupation with the past occurrence
		• Lingering feelings of discomfort, remorse, resentment, or regret
		• Awkward interpersonal relationships with those involved in the conflict
		• Distraction from tasks
		• Gossip
		• Relief
		• Denial
		• What else? ____
		  ____
		• ____
			• If conflict is viewed as bad, then its aftermath will be viewed negatively as well
			• Inability to let go of the past
			• Fear of repeat conflicts
			• Conflict was not addressed or resolved quickly or effectively
			• What else? ____
			  ____
			• ____
			• ____
				• Get team buy-in and commitment to focus constructively on future goals and lessons learned
				• Change team seating at meetings to encourage new relationship-building
				• Ask the team to recommend ways to manage its conflicts differently in the future
				• Conduct one-on-one interviews with team members to assess the impact
				• Refocus the team on a new issue or goal to address	

A.4 IDENTIFYING TEAM STAGES USING STARS®

TEMPLATE OVERVIEW	TEMPLATE PREPARATION	DATE
Determine the team's stage of development using an observation process called STARS.®	Prepared By:	
	Approved By:	

STARS® COMPONENT: "SAY" – What team members say to each other: content, tone, context, formality

TEAM STAGE	BEHAVIORS TO OBSERVE			COMMENTS
Forming (Orientation)	• Frequent "I" comments expressing individuality	□ YES	□ NO	
	• Uncertainty or anxiety expressed	□ YES	□ NO	
	• High-assertive individuals may say "we" but really mean "I" based on personal agendas	□ YES	□ NO	
	• Statements and questions showing uncertainty or caution	□ YES	□ NO	
Storming (Disorientation)	• "I" language attempting to represent strong team opinions without members' consent	□ YES	□ NO	
	• Defensive language emphasizing "you" vs. "me" and "us" vs. "them"	□ YES	□ NO	
	• Blaming people instead of the problem	□ YES	□ NO	
	• Passive-aggressive statements with a victimized mentality	□ YES	□ NO	

continued

STARS® COMPONENT: "SAY" – What team members say to each other: content, tone, context, formality

TEAM STAGE	BEHAVIORS TO OBSERVE			COMMENTS
Norming (Standardization)	• Words and phrases that team members use with each other for their own special language and mutual understanding	☐ YES	☐ NO	
	• Genuine "we" and "us" wording to express ideas for the team as a cohesive unit	☐ YES	☐ NO	
	• Supportive comments about/from team members to encourage different views about team processes	☐ YES	☐ NO	
	• Emphasis on mutual interests of all members: productivity, vision, values, challenges, and solutions	☐ YES	☐ NO	
Performing (Unification)	• Interchangeable and equal references to "I", "we", and "us"	☐ YES	☐ NO	
	• Self-assessment questions to improve interpersonally as a team such as, "How well did we argue?"	☐ YES	☐ NO	
	• References to the team vision with a sense of urgency and commitment	☐ YES	☐ NO	
	• Discussing risks to take as a team to learn, grow, and improve for better team performance	☐ YES	☐ NO	
Adjourning (Disbanding)	• Frequent references to the team as a family unit, using "us" and "we"	☐ YES	☐ NO	
	• Expressions of sadness and regret about the team disbanding soon	☐ YES	☐ NO	
	• Telling stories about shared team history and achievements	☐ YES	☐ NO	
	• "I" statements conveying individual anxiety and anticipation about the future	☐ YES	☐ NO	

Forming (Orientation)	Team members perform tasks collectively on a trial-and-error basis	☐ YES ☐ NO
	There is no formalized team process for how to assign, prioritize, and complete tasks	☐ YES ☐ NO
	Some people on the team do more work than others, indicating an unequal task distribution	☐ YES ☐ NO
	Emphasis is on individual task completion	☐ YES ☐ NO
Storming (Disorientation)	Personalities and politics influence team member discussions and priorities regarding workload distribution	☐ YES ☐ NO
	Team members attempt to create a process for task knowledge transfer despite differing viewpoints	☐ YES ☐ NO
	Team members disagree about individual methodologies and at times compete with each other for dominance	☐ YES ☐ NO
	Individuals can be defensive about asking "Why?" and "Why not?" related to individual task completion assignments	☐ YES ☐ NO
Norming (Standardization)	Team members settle into a routine of established procedures and guidelines for tasks	☐ YES ☐ NO
	Team members follow clearly defined processes for task knowledge transfer to strengthen team performance	☐ YES ☐ NO
	Team members begin to initiate formalized team processes to improve task quality and efficiency for all	☐ YES ☐ NO
	Team members assume individual accountability for task performance	☐ YES ☐ NO
	Team members are so comfortable with their own team processes and task methods that they can become resistant to new task approaches	☐ YES ☐ NO

continued

STARS® COMPONENT: "SAY" - What team members say to each other: content, tone, context, formality

TEAM STAGE	BEHAVIORS TO OBSERVE			COMMENTS
Performing (Unification)	• Team members share task roles and responsibilities interchangeably with equal levels of proficiency	☐ YES	☐ NO	
	• Team members consistently achieve and exceed task performance goals with high confidence and proficiency	☐ YES	☐ NO	
	• The team consistently demonstrates task knowledge transfer efficiency	☐ YES	☐ NO	
	• Team members challenge status quo standards for task performance and inspire each other to take risks to become more innovative	☐ YES	☐ NO	
Adjourning (Disbanding)	• Team members focus on completing all tasks before the team disbands	☐ YES	☐ NO	
	• The team finalizes documentation for archival purposes	☐ YES	☐ NO	
	• Team members can become distracted from completing tasks when they are preoccupied with saying good-bye and celebrating team achievements	☐ YES	☐ NO	
	• Team members explore future career options for working on a new team	☐ YES	☐ NO	
Forming (Orientation)	• Team members avoid arguing and disagreeing as much as possible	☐ YES	☐ NO	
	• Team members prefer not to argue over controversial issues	☐ YES	☐ NO	
	• Dominant members assert their views and are rarely challenged by nonassertive team members who want to keep the peace	☐ YES	☐ NO	

Storming (Disorientation)	• Individuals tend to argue against others who are different or do not conform to the most popular points of view	☐ YES	☐ NO
	• Team members demonstrate some passive-aggressive behaviors as their conflict styles	☐ YES	☐ NO
	• Dominant team members assert themselves while less assertive ones withdraw	☐ YES	☐ NO
Norming (Standardization)	• The team follows ground rules for acceptable behaviors and processes for discussing, debating and disagreeing, and deciding	☐ YES	☐ NO
	• The team has established a process for arguing that is beneficial to everyone	☐ YES	☐ NO
	• Norms for focusing on "us against the problem" vs. "us against each other" are accepted by team members	☐ YES	☐ NO
Performing (Unification)	• Team members engage in open discussion, debate, disagreement, and decision-making using a principled process that ensures full participation	☐ YES	☐ NO
	• Team members challenge their own processes and assumptions to ensure continuous improvement	☐ YES	☐ NO
	• The team has perfected its processes for effective conflict management	☐ YES	☐ NO
Adjourning (Disbanding)	• Team members challenge each other to convey different points of view about meeting final performance goals	☐ YES	☐ NO
	• The team collaborates on lessons learned	☐ YES	☐ NO
Forming (Orientation)	• Team members overuse consensus by trial-and-error as the primary form of agreement	☐ YES	☐ NO
	• The team does not have a formal process for agreement	☐ YES	☐ NO
	• Agreement on an individual's roles and responsibilities is more important than agreement on the team's needs as a cohesive unit	☐ YES	☐ NO

continued

STARS® COMPONENT: "SAY" - What team members say to each other: content, tone, context, formality

TEAM STAGE	BEHAVIORS TO OBSERVE			COMMENTS
Storming (Disorientation)	• The team has no process for agreement as a team, but members attempt to create one despite interpersonal differences	☐ YES	☐ NO	
	• Team members seek to influence others to agree based on politics and friendships	☐ YES	☐ NO	
	• The team can become divided based on interpersonal differences and tensions			
	• Team members speak out more for individual preferences than for the team			
Norming (Standardization)	• Team members have a process in place for reaching agreement after giving and receiving feedback constructively	☐ YES	☐ NO	
	• The team follows a collaborative process for mutual decision making based on performance requirements			
	• "Group think" can occur if team members become so settled that they agree with each other too much, and reject new ideas that contradict their norms and routines	☐ YES	☐ NO	
Performing (Unification)	• Team members focus more on identifying improvements through active disagreement than by seeking to agree just to appease others	☐ YES	☐ NO	
	• The team has established an effective process for conflict resolution involving accountability from everyone	☐ YES	☐ NO	
Adjourning (Disbanding)	• Team members share how they feel about the team disbanding	☐ YES	☐ NO	
	• The team finds meaningful ways to close out projects through active discussion and agreement on best ideas	☐ YES	☐ NO	

		YES/NO	
Forming (Orientation)	• Team members are uncertain about how to interact with each other as a unit	☐ YES ☐ NO	
	• Team members attempt to build rapport	☐ YES ☐ NO	
	• The team has no process for managing interpersonal relationship differences	☐ YES ☐ NO	
	• Trust has not yet been established among team members	☐ YES ☐ NO	
Storming (Disorientation)	• Team members attempt to gain acceptance and popularity. Some cliques and polarized groups can form as a result	☐ YES ☐ NO	
	• Some team members compete with others for more power and authority within the team	☐ YES ☐ NO	
	• Team members respond differently to diverse styles: some become more aggressive, some give in, and some withdraw	☐ YES ☐ NO	
Norming (Standardization)	• Team members demonstrate increased tolerance for different personality styles and attempt to adapt	☐ YES ☐ NO	
	• The team formalizes processes for working together as a cohesive unit with agreed-upon norms for acceptable and unacceptable behavior	☐ YES ☐ NO	
	• Team members demonstrate more effectiveness interpersonally to support and trust each other more	☐ YES ☐ NO	
Performing (Unification)	• Team members fully accept and encourage each other despite different styles	☐ YES ☐ NO	
	• Team members demonstrate mutual trust and respect despite differences of opinion and conflicts	☐ YES ☐ NO	
	• The team self-manages behaviors that negatively affect team relationships, such as gossiping or criticizing	☐ YES ☐ NO	

continued

STARS® COMPONENT: "SAY" – What team members say to each other: content, tone, context, formality

TEAM STAGE	BEHAVIORS TO OBSERVE			COMMENTS
Adjourning (Disbanding)	• Team members feel anxiety about the team disbanding and leaving close colleagues	☐ YES	☐ NO	
	• Team members feel the need to reaffirm and celebrate their close ties	☐ YES	☐ NO	
	• The team feels pride for its mutual accomplishments and has grown to "feel like a family"	☐ YES	☐ NO	
	• Individuals turn to each other for emotional support and networking advice for future career options on another team	☐ YES	☐ NO	
Forming (Orientation)	• Individual members define the "team" based on their own agendas and perceptions	☐ YES	☐ NO	
	• There is no agreed-upon perception of the team's identity as a unit	☐ YES	☐ NO	
	• The team does not yet have a clear perception of its collective talents, skills, and potential capabilities	☐ YES	☐ NO	
	• "Teamwork" is viewed more as individual task completion than as team processes for disagreement and innovation	☐ YES	☐ NO	
Storming (Disorientation)	• The group experiences growing pains from interpersonal tensions and conflicts arising from confusion about the team's identity as a unit	☐ YES	☐ NO	
	• Team members are so involved in their personal struggles to cope with the group that they do not yet have an accurate perception of the team's overall strengths and areas for development	☐ YES	☐ NO	
	• Team members lack a shared perception of the ideal team they would like to become	☐ YES	☐ NO	

Norming (Standardization)	• Team members begin to understand that a strong team is larger than the sum of its individual needs	□ YES	□ NO
	• The team has a clearer identity based understanding the vision, mission, and goals for the future	□ YES	□ NO
	• Team members begin to care more about how the team is perceived as a whole unit	□ YES	□ NO
Performing (Unification)	• The team perceives itself as self-reliant	□ YES	□ NO
	• Perceived values of risk-taking, innovation, and shared accountability unite team members	□ YES	□ NO
	• "Teamwork" is emphasized as challenging each other to achieve the team vision, mission, and goals for continuous improvement	□ YES	□ NO
Adjourning (Disbanding)	• The self-perception of team members is as a "family" unit	□ YES	□ NO
	• Individuals perceive that although the team is disbanding, they will remain linked emotionally and professionally in the future	□ YES	□ NO
	• Team membership is remembered as a privilege that fosters individual and collective growth	□ YES	□ NO

A.5 TEAM DEVELOPMENT PLAN TEMPLATE

TEMPLATE OVERVIEW	TEMPLATE PREPARATION	DATE
Prepare a team development plan efficiently for the purpose of guiding and managing the team's growth and performance.	**Prepared By:**	
	Approved By:	

TEAM DEVELOPMENT PLAN TEMPLATE

COMPONENT	DETAILS	COMMENTS
Purpose	• Identify the quantitative and qualitative measurements for assessing team performance at each stage of its development	
	• Itemize the tools, methods, and activities required to achieve performance deliverables at each stage in the team's life cycle	
	• Establish a vision for the team to strive for as it develops through all stages of the team life cycle	
	• Be proactive in developing the team to reach its full potential	
	• Provide a baseline for evaluating team progress	
	• Create a guide for directing and charting the deliberate course of action for developing the team	

Team Stage of Development	
Assessment	☐ Forming (Orientation)
	☐ Storming (Disorientation)
	☐ Norming (Standardization)
	☐ Performing (Unification)
	☐ Adjourning (Disbanding)
	Team Behaviors
	• Identify at least three positive team behaviors related to how tasks are assigned, prioritized, shared, improved, executed, and evaluated: ○ _____ ○ _____ ○ _____
	• Identify at least three team behaviors related to tasks that need to be improved, such as how tasks are assigned, prioritized, shared, improved, executed, or evaluated: ○ _____ ○ _____ ○ _____
	• Identify at least three positive team behaviors regarding how team members discuss, debate, disagree, decide, debrief, and generally relate to each other: ○ _____ ○ _____ ○ _____

continued

TEAM DEVELOPMENT PLAN TEMPLATE

COMPONENT	DETAILS	COMMENTS
Assessment (continued)	• Identify at least three team behaviors needing improvement regarding how team members discuss, debate, disagree, decide, debrief, and generally relate to each other: ○ _____ ○ _____ ○ _____	
Vision Statement (Future)	What is the future state of the team that represents its success as a cohesive unit? To consider as part of the team vision: core values, legacy to be remembered for, unique contribution to stakeholders and the marketplace, the impact the team wishes to make on the organization, customers, consumers, and others. Team Vision Statement: _____ _____ _____	
Mandate/Charter (Present)	What is the reason for the existence of the team at the present time, and what is the team's primary function, mandate, or charter? Team Mandate/Charter: _____ _____ _____	
Mission	How will the team achieve the vision in terms of its overall approach and priorities? Team Mission: _____ _____	

Goal	More specifically, what is the key aim or result that the team needs to complete to achieve its mission? Team Goal:
Deliverables	What specifically does the team need to deliver to achieve the team goal? Consider what, when, and where. Try to make the team deliverable statement "SMART": Specific, Measurable, Achievable, Realistic, and Time-activated. Team Deliverable(s):
"SWOT" Analysis	**S**trengths of the team: job-related knowledge, team processes and procedures, capabilities:
	Weaknesses of the team: areas for development, including performance, conflict and stress management, decision making, and problem solving:
	Opportunities external to the team: what can potentially help the team grow and succeed? Consider changes to the organization, market conditions, and technological changes:
	Threats external to the team: what can potentially harm the team's growth and development? Consider the impact of market conditions, economies, technology, and customer trends:

A.6 TEAM PERFORMANCE ACTION PLANNER

TEMPLATE OVERVIEW	TEMPLATE PREPARATION	DATE
Identify action steps for developing the team's competencies in task and relationship behaviors throughout all stages of the team's life cycle.	Prepared By:	
	Approved By:	

Tasks		
Team Development Stage	**Action Steps for Team Development**	**Comments**
Forming	Create a team website or central database for knowledge sharing	
	Generate a reference list of key terminology and acronyms for projects to encourage a common team language	
	Allocate a short time at team meetings for team members to communicate task knowledge on a rotating basis	
	Assign team members with different work styles or locations to collaborate on a project task	
Storming	Identify criteria to evaluate individual and team performance	
	Review the performance criteria individually and also with the entire team	
	Coach each team member on how to complete tasks more efficiently and effectively	
	Facilitate team brainstorming at meetings to generate ideas for knowledge transfer and ways to improve the team's overall task performance	
Norming	Assign short project challenges to help the team build problem-solving skills	
	Encourage peer reviews of tasks for knowledge sharing and collaboration	
	At team meetings, introduce new methodologies and processes for tasks to improve team knowledge and productivity	

Tasks		
Team Development Stage	**Action Steps for Team Development**	**Comments**
Norming (continued)	Conduct regular team training sessions and invite special subject-matter experts to develop team knowledge	
	Facilitate team discussion about how to improve knowledge transfer more consistently and efficiently	
Performing	Assign tasks to team members with less proficiency to build their skills to the same level for effective succession planning	
	At meetings, debrief team members on lessons learned for continuous improvement	
	Encourage the team to challenge its own task methods by testing more innovative approaches	
	Regularly rotate tasks to develop versatility among team members	
	Delegate an entire project for the team to manage with full control over performance goals, budget, and implementation	
Adjourning	Provide frequent opportunities for the team to celebrate their past successes as they prepare to disband for future opportunities on other teams	
	Regularly consult with team members for task progress updates before they adjourn	
Relationships		
Forming	Communicate and enforce ground rules for acceptable team behaviors	
	Allocate between 10% and 20% of meeting time for team members to build relationships by learning about each other's interests and views	
	Standardize the steps team members need to follow for discussion, debating, disagreeing, and deciding	
	Provide frequent opportunities for team members to exchange views and make small decisions	
	Brainstorm with team members to share their ideas, both publicly and anonymously	

continued

Tasks		
Team Development Stage	**Action Steps for Team Development**	**Comments**
Storming	Publicize ground rules for team behavioral norms at all meetings and other team events	
	Assign team members to discuss and debate topics regularly and provide constructive feedback on their interpersonal effectiveness	
	Coach individuals on interpersonal skills, including style awareness and adaptation, diplomacy, and conflict management	
	Appoint an external facilitator to observe a team discussion and provide constructive feedback	
Norming	Assign team members to lead segments of team meetings on a rotating basis to showcase different task approaches	
	Invite members to contribute new ideas for improving group processes for discussing, debating, disagreeing, and deciding	
	Initiate peer mentoring processes to encourage collaboration	
	Challenge the team to build working partnerships based on diversity, trust, and a shared team vision for the future	
Performing	Individually and collectively offer constructive feedback to team members regarding communication effectiveness	
	Challenge the team as a unit to enhance its flexibility and leadership skills	
	Rotate "team leaders" regularly and assign the team to give constructive feedback for improvement	
	Assign the team to reevaluate and improve its own internal processes for discussing, debating, disagreeing, and deciding	
Adjourning	Encourage the team to plan some of their own good-bye activities	
	Provide mentoring assistance to help team members overcome separation anxiety and plan for their futures on new teams	
	Assign team members to share memorable stories about the team's experiences with others	

A.7 SELLING THE TEAM DEVELOPMENT PLAN: INFLUENCING CONVERSATION TEMPLATE

TEMPLATE OVERVIEW
Prepare to have a powerful, influential conversation to sell the team development plan to stakeholders and senior management.

TEMPLATE PREPARATION	DATE
Prepared By:	
Approved By:	

Influencing Conversation Template
Who is the person you are going to talk to? _____
What do you want that person to be aware of that he/she may not have been aware of before your conversation?
What are this person's key work and/or personal interests? State your assumptions:
What can you emphasize in your message that will generate interest from that person?
What commitment do you want from this person as a result of your discussion? Make sure it is realistic and achievable after only one discussion (for instance, changing one's style, attitude, or approach is not typically achievable after a short discussion).
What action do you want the other person to take after hearing your message? Is it realistic and achievable?
Create your key message. It should be in sentence form, not bullet points.

A.8 COMMUNICATING THE TEAM DEVELOPMENT PLAN: CHECKLIST

TEMPLATE OVERVIEW	TEMPLATE PREPARATION	DATE
Identify specific leadership action steps for communicating values and processes related to the team development plan.	Prepared By:	
	Approved By:	

LEADERSHIP ACTION	FREQUENCY				NEEDS IMPROVEMENT	IDEAS AND COMMENTS
	1=NEVER	2=SOMETIMES	3=USUALLY	4=ALWAYS		
Print It Out Display the team vision, mission, and goals in visible places for all team members to see	☐	☐	☐	☐	☐ YES ☐ NO	
Strengthen It Politically Meet regularly with the project sponsor and other senior managers to gain support for the team's development	☐	☐	☐	☐	☐ YES ☐ NO	
Give It a Good Kick-Off Include relevant aspects of the team development plan, including the vision, mission, and goals	☐	☐	☐	☐	☐ YES ☐ NO	
Facilitate the Process Ensure that team interactions are facilitated consistently by balancing task and relationship activities at all meetings and discussions	☐	☐	☐	☐	☐ YES ☐ NO	

Deliver It Consistently Communicate information to team members about relevant performance metrics and processes to set expectations for performance	□	□	□	□	□ YES	□ NO
Debrief Frequently Discuss progress pertaining to team development processes, challenges, successes, and ideas for improvement with team members	□	□	□	□	□ YES	□ NO
Conduct Benchmarking Collect information external to the organization about best practices pertaining to team development planning and share it at team meetings	□	□	□	□	□ YES	□ NO
Celebrate Celebrate small successes with the team when milestones related to the team development plan are achieved	□	□	□	□	□ YES	□ NO

A.9 MODELING THE TEAM DEVELOPMENT PLAN

TEMPLATE OVERVIEW	TEMPLATE PREPARATION	DATE
Identify ways to demonstrate the Team Development Plan to reinforce its values and processes for team members to model its importance.	**Prepared By:**	
	Approved By:	

LEADERSHIP ACTION	FREQUENCY 1=NEVER	2=SOMETIMES	3=USUALLY	4=ALWAYS	NEEDS IMPROVEMENT		IDEAS AND COMMENTS
Communicate and enforce ground rules at every team meeting	☐	☐	☐	☐	☐ YES	☐ NO	
Introduce and document team processes for discussing, disagreeing, debating, and deciding	☐	☐	☐	☐	☐ YES	☐ NO	
Get coaching on team development planning	☐	☐	☐	☐	☐ YES	☐ NO	
Get observed when you interact with team members to address team development issues	☐	☐	☐	☐	☐ YES	☐ NO	
Give and solicit feedback on the team's developmental progress	☐	☐	☐	☐	☐ YES	☐ NO	
Adapt your communications style to demonstrate increased flexibility and adaptability to diverse styles and avoid favoring styles similar to yours	☐	☐	☐	☐	☐ YES	☐ NO	

A.10 LEADING MULTIPLE GENERATIONS ON TEAMS: COMPARISON CHART

TEMPLATE OVERVIEW	TEMPLATE PREPARATION	DATE
Identify and compare multi-generational differences among team members to learn how to adapt to lead them better.	Prepared By:	
	Approved By:	

Name	Eras Born (Approximate)	Motto	Why Work?	Preferred Leadership	Evaluating Performance	Values at Work	To Motivate
Matures, GI Generation, Silent Generation, Traditionalists	1909–1945	Follow the rules, learn to fit in, do your part, stay in line, and you'll do fine	• To survive and support the family • To build a career in one company • To give and receive loyalty	A Clear Chain of Command	Working hard within the hierarchy to prove oneself worthy of promotion	Stick with what you are committed to, be loyal, do your part and you will be looked after when you retire	Show your loyalty by making sacrifices for the common good
Baby Boomers, Zoomers	1946–1964	The most direct path to the top can be found by working long and hard to achieve your dreams	• To earn a good income • To make a difference • To demonstrate company loyalty	A Democratic Leader	Number of hours worked equals success: hard work pays off	Experience matters as a way of developing knowledge and expertise	Inspire me to add value by sharing my expertise and years of experience to make a difference for the company

continued

Name	Eras Born (Approximate)	Motto	Why Work?	Preferred Leadership	Evaluating Performance	Values at Work	To Motivate
Generation Xers, Baby Busters	1965–1979	Money is good, but control of my time for people I choose to spend it with is more important	• To pay the bills • To learn new skills • To demonstrate loyalty to individuals, not the company	An Influential Mentor	Get the job done on time and to the boss's and your satisfaction so you can do important things outside work	Do what you say and say what you do consistently, and without lying	Pay me to figure out a better way do it efficiently
New Millennials, Generation Y's, Echo Boomers, New Silent Generation	1980–1994	Don't waste time waiting for tomorrow when you can get it today	• To afford chosen lifestyles and hobbies • For social interaction • To become whatever one wants to be as quickly as possible	A Friendly and Flexible Coach	Productivity is doing things as fast as possible by working smarter to live better	Knowledge does not depend on one's experience, so one is entitled to ask questions and make suggestions	Tell me what you want/need, but let me decide how to do it. Give me peer testimonials for motivation

Team Name: _____

Team Member Work Values: _____

Other Notes: _____

Generations on Team: _____

Leadership Styles to Emphasize: _____

A.11 BUILDING A STRONGER MULTIGENERATIONAL TEAM: CHECKLIST

TEMPLATE OVERVIEW	TEMPLATE PREPARATION	DATE
Identify ways to build a stronger multigenerational team.	Prepared By:	
	Approved By:	

	NOTES	DONE
Consistently communicate the vision, mission, goals, and deliverables through a variety of media, especially visually, in meeting rooms, prominently in emails, on intranet sites, and using social media		
Incorporate the Four M's at all team interactions:		
1. Make sure everyone knows and follows the ground rules for courteous and appropriate behavior (Matures)		
2. Make it worthwhile to give input and share best practices (Baby Boomers)		
3. Make it efficient to save time (Gen Xers)		
4. Make it motivating to feel appreciated (New Millennials)		
Implement an awareness program to acknowledge the unique contributions of each team member		
Establish a "buddy" system to pair different generations to share special skills and strengths		
Coach members individually on ways to "influence" others effectively based on common team goals		
Provide training opportunities to develop assertiveness, diplomacy, and influencing skills		

continued

	NOTES	DONE
Rotate multigenerational team members' roles at meetings and other team activities to showcase individual talents and approaches		
Model multigenerational communications competency as the leader by demonstrating an understanding and appreciation for each generation's uniqueness		
Provide reading materials and resources on generational diversity		
Ask for feedback to find out how you can model multigenerational synergies		

A.12 FACILITATING TEAM DEVELOPMENT AT MEETINGS

TEMPLATE OVERVIEW	TEMPLATE PREPARATION	DATE
Evaluate meeting facilitation readiness and effectiveness.	Prepared By:	
	Approved By:	

Meeting Facilitation Skills	COMPETENCY			COMMENTS
Announce and enforce ground rules for acceptable and unacceptable behaviors	1 Low	2 Med	3 High	
Remain "neutral" in point of view; you are the catalyst, not the key focus	1 Low	2 Med	3 High	
Create a "Parking Lot" for details to be addressed later	1 Low	2 Med	3 High	
Summarize key points and make them visual	1 Low	2 Med	3 High	
Help the group stay focused on the outcomes	1 Low	2 Med	3 High	
Establish and encourage a group process for disagreeing without arguing	1 Low	2 Med	3 High	
Establish and encourage a group process for making key decisions	1 Low	2 Med	3 High	
Summarize what was suggested	1 Low	2 Med	3 High	
Encourage active participation from everyone	1 Low	2 Med	3 High	
Create and maintain a positive team climate	1 Low	2 Med	3 High	

continued

Meeting Facilitation Skills	COMPETENCY			COMMENTS
Ensure that all three learning styles are addressed (hearing, seeing, doing)	1 Low	2 Med	3 High	
Get commitment and agreement on next steps before the meeting ends	1 Low	2 Med	3 High	
Break teams into sub-groups at times to enhance participation	1 Low	2 Med	3 High	
Encourage, affirm, support, repeat, ask "what-if" questions, rephrase key ideas	1 Low	2 Med	3 High	
End with a positive statement	1 Low	2 Med	3 High	

A.13 THE 4Ds PLANNING TEMPLATE

TEMPLATE OVERVIEW	TEMPLATE PREPARATION	DATE
Acquire a list of questions to answer to ensure that the team follows an effective process for discussing, disagreeing, debating, and deciding (The 4D's).	Prepared By:	
	Approved By:	

		Process	Notes
Discussing		• Communicate the ground rules for discussing	
		• Gain team commitment to follow the ground rules	
		• Establish a group process for how and when team members will contribute individual ideas and ensure that they are heard nonjudgmentally	
		• Establish rules and responsibilities, including scribe, timekeeper, and minute taker	
Debating		• Determine the team process to use for disagreeing without escalating into conflict	
		• Communicate the team process for disagreement and debate	
		• Manage the team process to avoid dominant members from taking over or nonassertive members from withdrawing	
		• Gain commitment from team members to be accountable for and listening to and contributing to differing viewpoints	
Deciding		• Determine the methods and processes the team will use to make decisions (e.g., voting, numerical ranking, decision tree)	
		• Gain commitment from team members to follow the process	
		• Identify ways to ensure that the impact of decisions on the business, stakeholders, the project, and the team is addressed	
		• Agree on how the decision will be documented and assign roles and responsibilities	
Debriefing		• Review lessons learned and ideas for improving team processes next time for discussing, debating, deciding, and debriefing	

A.14 BUILDING TEAM COLLABORATION CHECKLIST

TEMPLATE OVERVIEW	TEMPLATE PREPARATION	DATE
Identify ways to build team collaboration using language, problem solving, and influence.	Prepared By:	
	Approved By:	

Team Vision Statement: _____
_____
_____

Team's Common Interests (Select all that apply)

☐ Customer Satisfaction	☐ Quality	☐ Reputation	☐ Recognition	☐ Pride	☐ Status
☐ Achievement	☐ Innovation	☐ Efficiency	☐ Teamwork	☐ Security	☐ Other

Specify "Other": _____
_____
_____

Team Collaboration Action Steps	Comments
Identify and communicate the team's common interest	
Gain team commitment to the common interest	
Communicate ground rules and processes for generating ideas	
Encourage team members to communicate assertively and diplomatically	
Ask team members to think and say "and" instead of "but"	
Emphasize thinking, speaking, and writing in the "aim frame" instead of the "blame frame"	
Focus discussions on future solutions, instead of past problems	
Create a safe, problem-solving environment where team members are supported to demonstrate "us against the problem" options and solutions through active writing and idea sharing	

A.15 TEAM MEETING FACILITATION BEST PRACTICES CHECKLIST

Best Practice	Yes: Was Observed	No: Was Not Observed
Ground rules posted		
Note taker assigned		
Process for agreement and disagreement		
Process for acknowledging speakers and hearing everyone's views		
Agenda reviewed		
Action steps posted/written down/read for who/when/what to follow up		
Timekeeper kept on track		
Expected contribution from all participants was clear		
Balanced participation from all		
Seating assignments encouraged open discussion from all		
Leader maintained control of participants' tone and content to ensure it was in "aim frame" instead of "blame frame"		
Leader discouraged side-bar conversations		

A.16 TEAM STAGES AND ACTIVITY GOALS

Team Stage	Activity Goal
Forming	Develop awareness of others and build trust
Storming	Help members tolerate and accept differences
Norming	Encourage team collaboration to improve tasking and relating processes
Performing	Support team self-sufficiency for process improvement
Adjourning	Assist with team celebration and archiving of achievements using best practices

Notes:

A.17 TEAM COMPETENCY NEEDS

Team Name:	
Description:	
Purpose:	
Team Mission/Vision:	
Key Projects/Priorities:	
Goal(s): Short-Term (up to 2 years):	
Goal(s): Long-Term (3 to 5 years):	

	Specific short-term and long-term needs the team will address:	**Priority**		
a.	Knowledge Transfer:	□ High	□ Medium	□ Low
b.	Skill Development:	□ High	□ Medium	□ Low
c.	Ability Contribution:	□ High	□ Medium	□ Low
d.	Feedback:	□ High	□ Medium	□ Low
e.	Budget Summary/ROI:	□ High	□ Medium	□ Low
All or parts of the project charter and human resources, communication, and/or organizational succession plans (if applicable)				

A.18 EVALUATING THE TEAM "BRAIN" OF KNOWLEDGE: CHECKLIST

TEMPLATE OVERVIEW	TEMPLATE PREPARATION	DATE
Assess the team's collective knowledge and competencies regarding people, team processes, and technology for succession planning purposes.	Prepared By:	
	Approved By:	

TEAM KNOWLEDGE AREA	PROFICIENCY				NEEDS IMPROVEMENT	COMMENTS
	1=NEVER	2=SOMETIMES	3=USUALLY	4=ALWAYS		
People						
Sharing knowledge of the needs and perspectives of:						
• Stakeholders	□	□	□	□	□ YES □ NO	
• Senior management	□	□	□	□	□ YES □ NO	
• Customers	□	□	□	□	□ YES □ NO	
• Vendors	□	□	□	□	□ YES □ NO	
• Team members	□	□	□	□	□ YES □ NO	

Communication Effectiveness

Conveying shared information clearly to:	1=NEVER	2=SOMETIMES	3=USUALLY	4=ALWAYS		
• Stakeholders	☐	☐	☐	☐	☐ YES	☐ NO
• Senior management	☐	☐	☐	☐	☐ YES	☐ NO
• Customers	☐	☐	☐	☐	☐ YES	☐ NO
• Vendors	☐	☐	☐	☐	☐ YES	☐ NO
• Team members	☐	☐	☐	☐	☐ YES	☐ NO
Sharing knowledge of how to get buy-in and commitment by negotiating and influencing:	1=NEVER	2=SOMETIMES	3=USUALLY	4=ALWAYS		
• Stakeholders	☐	☐	☐	☐	☐ YES	☐ NO
• Senior management	☐	☐	☐	☐	☐ YES	☐ NO
• Customers	☐	☐	☐	☐	☐ YES	☐ NO
• Vendors	☐	☐	☐	☐	☐ YES	☐ NO
• Team members	☐	☐	☐	☐	☐ YES	☐ NO

continued

TEAM KNOWLEDGE AREA	PROFICIENCY				NEEDS IMPROVEMENT		COMMENTS
	1=NEVER	2=SOMETIMES	3=USUALLY	4=ALWAYS			
Team processes							
Sharing knowledge about team processes for:							
• Tasks	☐	☐	☐	☐	☐ YES	☐ NO	
• Administration	☐	☐	☐	☐	☐ YES	☐ NO	
• Budgeting	☐	☐	☐	☐	☐ YES	☐ NO	
• Meetings	☐	☐	☐	☐	☐ YES	☐ NO	
• Project management	☐	☐	☐	☐	☐ YES	☐ NO	
• Business analysis	☐	☐	☐	☐	☐ YES	☐ NO	
• Information transfer	☐	☐	☐	☐	☐ YES	☐ NO	
• Other (specify): _____ _____	☐	☐	☐	☐	☐ YES	☐ NO	
Technology							
Internal: Within the organization	1=NEVER	2=SOMETIMES	3=USUALLY	4=ALWAYS			
• Information Technology systems	☐	☐	☐	☐	☐ YES	☐ NO	
• Information Technology processes	☐	☐	☐	☐	☐ YES	☐ NO	

	1=NEVER	2=SOMETIMES	3=USUALLY	4=ALWAYS			
• Project-related software	☐	☐	☐	☐		☐ YES	☐ NO
• Terminology and acronyms	☐	☐	☐	☐		☐ YES	☐ NO
• Project management	☐	☐	☐	☐		☐ YES	☐ NO
• Business analysis	☐	☐	☐	☐		☐ YES	☐ NO
• Other (specify): _____	☐	☐	☐	☐		☐ YES	☐ NO
External: Outside the organization							
• Information Technology systems	☐	☐	☐	☐		☐ YES	☐ NO
• Information Technology processes	☐	☐	☐	☐		☐ YES	☐ NO
• Project-related software	☐	☐	☐	☐		☐ YES	☐ NO
• Terminology and acronyms	☐	☐	☐	☐		☐ YES	☐ NO
• Project management	☐	☐	☐	☐		☐ YES	☐ NO
• Business analysis	☐	☐	☐	☐		☐ YES	☐ NO
• Other (specify): _____	☐	☐	☐	☐		☐ YES	☐ NO

A.19 TEAM TRANSFORMATION GUIDELINES

TEMPLATE OVERVIEW	TEMPLATE PREPARATION	DATE
Identify ten key steps to follow to guide the team throughout the transformation process.	Prepared By:	
	Approved By:	

TEAM NAME	
TEAM PROJECT(S)	

TEAM TRANSFORMATION GUIDELINE	FREQUENCY			COMMENTS
1a. The team sees the vision posted in key meeting locations and other visible areas	1 Low	2 Med	3 High	
1b. The team hears the vision stated at every meeting and at other team events	1 Low	2 Med	3 High	
1c. The team is encouraged to apply the vision to the transformation process	1 Low	2 Med	3 High	
2. The team observes senior executive leaders modeling the vision for the future	1 Low	2 Med	3 High	
3. Team members learn from the senior executive leaders and team leader what transformational changes need to be made and why	1 Low	2 Med	3 High	
4. Team members know and practice operating norms for new behaviors to demonstrate for the transformation	1 Low	2 Med	3 High	
5. Team members know what new processes and performance standards are required for all to follow	1 Low	2 Med	3 High	

TEAM TRANSFORMATION GUIDELINE	FREQUENCY			COMMENTS
6. Team members have input in creating and updating the team charter to incorporate the transformational vision and goals	1 Low	2 Med	3 High	
7. Team members are encouraged to share knowledge and skills considered essential for achieving the transformation	1 Low	2 Med	3 High	
8a. Team members have opportunities to recommend new ideas and processes for achieving the transformation	1 Low	2 Med	3 High	
8b. Team members are updated about which suggestions and ideas will be implemented to help achieve the transformation	1 Low	2 Med	3 High	
9. The team has opportunities to discuss transformational challenges and evaluate progress achieving specific performance goals and standards	1 Low	2 Med	3 High	
10. Team members are challenged to identify new ways to explore, expand, execute, and redefine the vision so they have ownership of the transformation process	1 Low	2 Med	3 High	
11. The team celebrates milestones regularly to stay motivated and informed about progress made to achieve the transformation	1 Low	2 Med	3 High	
12. The team is encouraged regularly to develop a collaborative mindset as a unified "community"	1 Low	2 Med	3 High	

A.20 TEAM TRANSFORMATION SKILL DEVELOPMENT PLANNER

TEMPLATE OVERVIEW
Plan for the team development of core skills needed to achieve the transformation successfully.

TEMPLATE PREPARATION	DATE
Prepared By:	
Approved By:	

TEAM NAME	
TEAM PROJECT(S)	

TEAM TRANSFORMATION GUIDELINE						Next Steps
Tolerance of Ambiguity	1 = NEVER - - - 5 = ALWAYS					
The team handles ambiguous or missing information without frustration or hesitation	☐	☐	☐	☐	☐	
The team is able to see the bigger picture beyond missing, inconsistent, or incomplete details	☐	☐	☐	☐	☐	
The team has confidence to make decisions based on contradictory or vague information	☐	☐	☐	☐	☐	
Flexible Thinking and Problem-Solving Skills						
The team demonstrates a variety of thinking styles:	1 = NEVER - - - 5 = ALWAYS					
Strategic planning	☐	☐	☐	☐	☐	
Analytical reasoning	☐	☐	☐	☐	☐	
Creative insights	☐	☐	☐	☐	☐	
Tactical abilities	☐	☐	☐	☐	☐	
Administrative processes	☐	☐	☐	☐	☐	
Operational processes	☐	☐	☐	☐	☐	

TEAM TRANSFORMATION GUIDELINE						Next Steps
The team uses both sides of the brain to solve problems	**1 = NEVER - - - 5 = ALWAYS**					
Left Side (Logical, Sequential, Linear)	□	□	□	□	□	
Right Side (Intuitive, Spontaneous, Nonlinear)	□	□	□	□	□	
Influencing Expertise	**1 = NEVER - - - 5 = ALWAYS**					
The team is effective influencing upward to senior management and sponsors	□	□	□	□	□	
The team is effective influencing colleagues and others with similar job titles and functions	□	□	□	□	□	
Emotional Intelligence for Resiliency	**1 = NEVER - - - 5 = ALWAYS**					
The team is self-aware of its stage of development and what action is needed to progress to the next stage	□	□	□	□	□	
The team is able to self-assess how its members react to conflict and manage tendencies to give up or get even by focusing on the issues, not the personalities	□	□	□	□	□	
Team members exhibit resiliency in dealing with challenges, changes, and disappointments	□	□	□	□	□	
Team members are unified in focusing on overcoming obstacles of the past to achieve the goals for future transformation	□	□	□	□	□	
Calculated Risk-Taking	**1 = NEVER - - - 5 = ALWAYS**					
The team uses an effective process for testing assumptions and challenging members to contribute new ideas for risk-taking opportunities	□	□	□	□	□	
The team acquires and transfers knowledge effectively for the purpose of preparing for future transformation	□	□	□	□	□	

continued

TEAM TRANSFORMATION GUIDELINE	1 = NEVER - - - 5 = ALWAYS					Next Steps
Team members demonstrate an entrepreneurial mindset that seeks to develop new processes and prototypes to achieve transformation competitively in the marketplace	☐	☐	☐	☐	☐	
Intercultural Communication Competence						
Team members demonstrate effective communications with cultures that are the following:	1 = NEVER - - - 5 = ALWAYS					
Low Context: valuing individuality, order, consistency, written documentation	☐	☐	☐	☐	☐	
High Context: valuing collectivism, spontaneity, trust, and oral traditions	☐	☐	☐	☐	☐	
The team discusses how to improve communications to have a global appeal to stakeholders from diverse cultures	☐	☐	☐	☐	☐	
Facilitating Knowledge Exchange	1 = NEVER - - - 5 = ALWAYS					
All team members receive continuous training and feedback on ways to facilitate meaningful dialogues to discuss how to achieve the transformation goals	☐	☐	☐	☐	☐	
Team meetings regarding the transformation are facilitated using ground rules and norms for behavior	☐	☐	☐	☐	☐	
The team is effective in discussing, debating, and deciding how to achieve the transformation	☐	☐	☐	☐	☐	

A.21 TEAM SUCCESSION PLANNING TEMPLATE

TEMPLATE OVERVIEW	TEMPLATE PREPARATION	DATE
Identify key questions to answer when creating a team succession plan for a transformation to be achieved.	Prepared By:	
	Approved By:	

TEAM NAME	
TEAM PROJECT(S)	

TEAM VISION FOR THE FUTURE:

Questions	Current State	Future State
What is the team's primary function/purpose?		
What job titles/functions comprise the team?		
How many people are on the team?		
Where are team members located?		
What new opportunities, technologies, and challenges are most influential for the team's success?		
What are the key 3–5 skills required for the team to succeed?	1.	1.
	2.	2.
	3.	3.
	4.	4.
	5.	5.

continued

Questions	Current State	Future State
Who are the key people with high potential for promotion?	To address current requirements	To address future requirements
	1.	1.
	2.	2.
	3.	3.
	4.	4.
	5.	5.
What training is needed for those high potentials to succeed?		
Technological Expertise		
Subject-Matter Knowledge		
Leadership and Communication Skills		
Other Skills (Specify:) _____ _____		
What processes are needed for back-up in case of changes or absences in team membership?		
What processes are needed for documenting changes for team knowledge sharing?		

A.22 PREPARING FOR THE FUTURE: TEAM DEVELOPMENT CHECKLIST

TEMPLATE OVERVIEW	TEMPLATE PREPARATION	DATE
Assist in identifying the team's current development level and what needs improvement to be more prepared to achieve transformation goals.	Prepared By:	
	Approved By:	

TEAM NAME	
TEAM PROJECT(S)	

			NEXT STEPS	
SKILLS FOR THE FUTURE	COMPETENCY		ACTION	DUE DATE
Self-Reliance: To question the status quo and initiate changes	1 Low	2 Med	3 High		
Managing Ambiguity: To make assumptions and cope with inconsistent information to remain focused on the vision and goals	1 Low	2 Med	3 High		
Coaching and Mentoring: Team members coach and mentor:					
Customers, vendors, business partners, and colleagues effectively	1 Low	2 Med	3 High		
Other project team colleagues	1 Low	2 Med	3 High		
Direct reports	1 Low	2 Med	3 High		

continued

		NEXT STEPS	
SKILLS FOR THE FUTURE	**COMPETENCY**	**ACTION**	**DUE DATE**
Mediation Expertise: Team members:			
Prevent conflicts from escalating among team partners	1 Low 2 Med 3 High		
Address conflicts proactively by exploring diverse perspectives and priorities	1 Low 2 Med 3 High		
Resolve conflicts effectively to accommodate all team partners	1 Low 2 Med 3 High		
Business Management Mindset: To have expertise from a business perspective beyond subject matter knowledge	1 Low 2 Med 3 High		
Strategic Thinking Capabilities: To focus on the team vision and goals	1 Low 2 Med 3 High		
Creativity: To demonstrate an inventive and intuitive approach to team problem-solving	1 Low 2 Med 3 High		
Interpersonal Intelligence: To show direction in building positive relationships through planned communications interactions	1 Low 2 Med 3 High		
Proactive about Succession Planning: To develop a broad base of skills in business management and technical areas	1 Low 2 Med 3 High		
Intercultural Communications Competence: To continuously seeks ways to interact effectively with diverse global stakeholders	1 Low 2 Med 3 High		

Selected Bibliography

Allen, David. *Getting Things Done: The Art of Stress-Free Productivity,* Toronto: Penguin Books, 2001.

Caroselli, Marlene. *Influence with Integrity: Power, Principles, and Persuasion*, Amherst, MA: HRD Press, 2000.

Davies, Anna, Devin Fidler, and Marina Gorbis. "Future Work Skills 2020," Institute for the Future for the University of Phoenix Research Institute, 2011, <http://www.slideshare.net/easa71/2020-future-work-skills-by-institute-of-the-future-pdf> (Accessed February 2, 2012).

Feldman, Daniel A. *The Manager's Pocket Guide to Workplace Coaching*, Amherst, MA: HRD Press, 2001.

Fogg, Davis C. *Team-Based Strategic Planning: A Complete Guide to Structuring, Facilitating and Implementing the Process*, New York: AMACOM, 1994.

Gallagher, Richard S. *How to Tell Anyone Anything: Breakthrough Techniques for Handling Difficult Conversations at Work,* New York: AMACOM, 2009.

Goleman, Daniel, Richard Boyatzis, and Annie McKee. *Primal Leadership: Learning to Lead with Emotional Intelligence*, Boston, MA: Harvard Business School Press, 2004.

Hall, Edward L. *Beyond Culture*, New York: Anchor Books, 1981.

Hamlin, Sonya. *How to Talk So People Listen. Connecting in Today's Workplace,* New York: HarperCollins Publishers, 2006.

Harvard Business School Staff. *Leading Teams: Expert Solutions to Everyday Challenges,* Harvard Business Review, reprinted January 2007.

Harvard Business School Staff. *Managing Knowledge to Fuel Growth*, Boston: Harvard Business School Press, 2007.

Harvard Business School Staff. *Managing Up. Expert Solutions to Everyday Challenges.* Boston: Harvard Business School Publishing Corporation, 2008.

Harvard Business School Staff. *Running Meetings. Expert Solutions to Everyday Challenges,* Boston: Harvard Business School Publishing, 2006.

Hayashi, Shawn Kent. *Conversations for Change. 12 Ways to Say It Right When It Matters Most,* New York: McGraw-Hill, 2011.

Hughes, Marcia, and James Bradford Terrell. *The Emotionally Intelligent Team. Understanding and Developing the Behaviors of Success*, San Francisco, CA: Jossey-Bass, 2007.

IBM Corporation Staff. *Working Beyond Borders: Insights from the Global Chief Human Resource Officer Study*, IBM Corporation, 2010. <http://public.dhe.ibm.com/comm> (accessed February 2, 2012).

International Business Institute. *A Guide to the Business Analysis Body of Knowledge® (BABOK® Guide)*, Toronto: International Institute of Business Analysis, 2009.

Juli, Thomas. *Leadership Principles for Project Success*, Boca Raton, FL: CRC Press, 2011.

Kotter, John P. *Leading Change. Why Transformation Efforts Fail*, Harvard Business Review article #R0701J-PDF-ENG, published January 1, 2007,

Lencioni, Patrick. *The Five Dysfunctions of a Team: A Leadership Fable*, San Francisco, CA: Jossey-Bass, 2002.

Lencioni, Patrick. *Overcoming the Five Dysfunctions of a Team: A Field Guide for Leaders, Managers, and Facilitators,* San Francisco, CA: Jossey-Bass, 2005.

Lancaster, Lynne C., and David Stillman. *When Generations Collide: Who They Are. Why They Clash. How to Solve the Generational Puzzle at Work,* New York: Collins Business, 2005.

Lynn, Adele B. *Quick Emotional Intelligence Activities for Busy Managers. 50 Team Exercises That Get Results in Just 15 Minutes,* New York, AMACOM, 2007.

Marston, Cam. *Motivating the "What's In It For Me?" Workforce: Manage Across the Generational Divide and Increase Profits,* Hoboken, NJ: John Wiley & Sons, Inc., 2007.

McManus, Patty. *Coaching People: Expert Solutions to Everyday Challenges,* Boston: Harvard Business School Publishing Corporation, 2006.

Mersino, Anthony. *Emotional Intelligence for Project Managers. The People Skills You Need to Achieve Outstanding Results,* New York: AMACOM, 2007.

Patterson, Kerry, Joseph Grenny, Ron McMillan, and Al Switzler. *Crucial Conversations: Tools for Talking When Stakes Are High,* New York: McGraw-Hill, 2002.

Pope, Sara. *The Manager's Pocket Guide to Team Sponsorship,* Amherst, MA: HRD Press and Minneapolis, MN: Lakewood Publications, 1998.

Project Management Institute®. *A Guide to the Project Management Body of Knowledge®* (*PMBOK® Guide*), fourth ed., Newtown Square, PA: Project Management Institute, Inc., 2008.

Project Management Institute®. *Project Management Circa 2025.* Ed. David Cleland and Bopaya Bidanda. Newtown Square, PA: Project Management Institute, Inc., 2009.

Schienle, Kathleen. *Achieving Goals: Define and Surpass Your High Performance Goals,* Irvington, NY: Hylas Publishing, 2007.

Templar, Richard. *How to Get What You Want Without Having to Ask,* Harlow, England: Prentice Hall Life, 2011.

Verma, Vijay. *Managing the Project Team,* Upper Darby, PA: Project Management Institute, 1997.

Wilkinson, David J. *The Ambiguity Advantage: What Great Leaders Are Great At,* Houndsmills, England: Palgrave MacMillan, 2006.

Index